Tailoring Prompts For Success - The Ultimate ChatGPT Prompt Engineering Guide

Michael Ferguson

Published by Michael Ferguson, 2023.

While every precaution has been taken in the preparation of this book, the publisher assumes no responsibility for errors or omissions, or for damages resulting from the use of the information contained herein.

TAILORING PROMPTS FOR SUCCESS - THE ULTIMATE CHATGPT PROMPT ENGINEERING GUIDE

First edition. April 17, 2023.

Copyright © 2023 Michael Ferguson.

ISBN: 979-8223575238

Written by Michael Ferguson.

Table of Contents

Chapter 1: Unlocking the Power Within: Understanding the Art of Prompt Engineering for Effective Interaction with ChatGPT 1

Chapter 2: Crafting Your Blueprint: Designing Specific and Unambiguous Prompts 9

Chapter 3: Refining Your Approach: Strategies for Iterative Prompt Engineering 17

Chapter 4: Igniting Creativity: Inspiring Unique and Imaginative Responses from ChatGPT 25

Chapter 5: Mastering Tone and Style: Crafting Nuanced Prompts for Desired Outputs 37

Conclusion 45

Chapter 1: Unlocking the Power Within: Understanding the Art of Prompt Engineering for Effective Interaction with ChatGPT

———

Welcome, dear reader, to the transformative journey of unlocking the power within you to effectively interact with ChatGPT, the cutting-edge language model. In this chapter, we will delve into the fascinating world of prompt engineering and explore practical strategies, expert techniques, and proven methods that will enable you to harness the full potential of ChatGPT for achieving your desired outcomes. Through well-researched content, relatable examples, and empowering exercises, you will gain the knowledge and skills to master the art of prompting and unlock a new level of interaction with this powerful AI technology.

As we embark on this journey together, let us first establish a clear and defined purpose for our exploration. The purpose of this chapter is to equip you with the tools and insights needed to optimize your interactions with ChatGPT, align your prompts with its capabilities, refine them for accuracy, inspire creativity, and achieve your writing goals. Whether you are a writer, a content creator, a marketer, or simply someone interested in utilizing ChatGPT for various purposes, this chapter will provide you with valuable insights and practical strategies for unlocking the power within you to effectively engage with this cutting-edge language model.

To ensure that the content of this chapter is based on well-researched principles and best practices, I have extensively studied the field of natural language processing, artificial intelligence, and human-computer interaction. I have also consulted with experts in the field and drawn on my own personal experiences and learnings from working with ChatGPT. The strategies and techniques shared in this chapter are based on a solid foundation of research and practical application, and I am excited to share them with you.

Crafting specific and unambiguous prompts is the cornerstone of effective prompt engineering. Your prompts serve as instructions to ChatGPT, guiding it to generate the desired output. Ambiguous prompts can result in inaccurate or irrelevant responses, while specific prompts can yield more precise and meaningful results. To craft effective prompts, consider the following strategies:

Clearly define your objective: Before formulating your prompt, be clear about your objective. What do you want to achieve with ChatGPT? Is it to generate ideas, draft content, or get answers to specific questions? Defining your objective will help you create prompts that align with your intended outcome.

Use clear and concise language: Clarity is crucial in prompt engineering. Use simple and concise language to communicate your instruction to ChatGPT. Avoid jargon, complex sentence structures, or ambiguous phrases that may confuse the model.

Specify desired format or structure: If you have a specific format or structure in mind for the output, include it in your prompt. For example, if you want ChatGPT to generate a list, specify that in your instruction. This helps guide the model to produce the desired output.

Include relevant context: Providing context in your prompts can help ChatGPT understand the context of your request and generate more relevant responses. Include relevant information, such as relevant keywords, background information, or relevant examples to help guide the model.

Experiment and iterate: Prompt engineering is an iterative process. Experiment with different prompts and iterate based on the results. Keep refining and optimizing your prompts to achieve better outcomes.

Now that you have crafted specific and unambiguous prompts, it's time to refine your approach to prompt engineering. This involves strategizing how to get the best results from ChatGPT by iterating and optimizing your prompts. Consider the following strategies:

Test different prompt variations: Experiment with different variations of prompts to explore the capabilities of ChatGPT. Try different sentence structures, wording, or context to see how it impacts the model's responses. Keep track of the results and iterate accordingly to refine your prompts for better outcomes.

Utilize system messages: System messages are a powerful tool in prompt engineering. They allow you to set the behavior of ChatGPT at the beginning of the conversation, guiding its responses throughout the interaction. Use system messages to gently instruct the model, provide context, or set the tone for the conversation.

Provide feedback: ChatGPT learns from feedback. If you get a response that is not aligned with your intended outcome, provide feedback to the model. You can do this by simply stating that the response is not what you were looking for or by rephrasing your prompt to be more explicit. ChatGPT can learn from this feedback and generate better responses in the future.

Experiment with temperature and max tokens: Temperature and max tokens are parameters that can be adjusted to influence the output of ChatGPT. Temperature controls the randomness of the responses, with higher values making the output more random, and lower values making it more focused and deterministic. Max tokens limit the length of the response. Experiment with these parameters to fine-tune the output to your liking.

Be mindful of ethical considerations: As with any technology, ethical considerations are important when using ChatGPT. Avoid prompts that encourage harmful, unethical, or biased behavior. Be mindful of the potential for biased responses from the model and take steps to mitigate it. Use ChatGPT in a responsible and ethical manner to ensure positive outcomes.

Now that you have a solid understanding of prompt engineering strategies and techniques, let's explore some practical examples of how you can implement these strategies in your interactions with ChatGPT.

Imagine you are a content creator working on a blog post about healthy eating. You want to use ChatGPT to generate ideas for healthy breakfast recipes. Instead of using a vague prompt like "Give me some healthy breakfast ideas," you can refine your prompt using the strategies we discussed earlier. Here's an example of a more specific and optimized prompt:

"ChatGPT, I am working on a blog post about healthy eating and I need your help to generate some creative and delicious breakfast recipes. Please provide me with three unique recipes that are easy to prepare, use wholesome ingredients, and are suitable for a vegan diet. Thank you!"

In this prompt, you have clearly defined your objective (to generate breakfast recipes), used clear and concise language, specified the desired format (three recipes), included relevant context (healthy eating, vegan diet), and provided feedback on the type of recipes you are looking for (creative, delicious, and easy to prepare). This optimized prompt is more likely to yield accurate and relevant results from ChatGPT.

As you engage with ChatGPT, remember to be mindful of the responses and critically evaluate the generated content. While ChatGPT is a powerful tool, it is still an AI model and may not always produce perfect results. Use your judgment to assess the quality and accuracy of the responses and make necessary adjustments to your prompts or instructions.

Empowerment and motivation are key elements in unlocking the power within you to effectively interact with ChatGPT. Believe in your ability to optimize your prompts, refine your approach, and achieve your desired outcomes. Embrace the creative potential of ChatGPT and use it as a tool to enhance your writing, content creation, or problem-solving skills. Remember that you are in control of the prompts you craft and the outcomes you achieve. With practice, patience, and persistence, you can unlock the full potential of ChatGPT and achieve remarkable results.

To further empower you on this journey, I have included a series of exercises for self-reflection and application. These exercises are designed to help you practice the prompt engineering strategies and techniques discussed in this chapter and apply them to real-life scenarios. Take the time to complete these exercises and reflect on how they can be applied to your specific use case with ChatGPT. Remember to be honest with yourself and open to learning from the process.

Exercise 1: Prompt Refinement

Take a prompt that you have used with ChatGPT in the past and analyze it using the prompt engineering strategies and techniques discussed in this chapter. Consider the following questions:

Is the objective of the prompt clear and well-defined?

Is the language of the prompt concise and specific?

Does the prompt provide relevant context or instructions?

Does the prompt include feedback or guidance for the desired output?

Can the prompt be optimized to be more specific or effective?

Based on your analysis, revise and refine the prompt to make it more effective in achieving your desired outcome. Experiment with different variations and observe the results from ChatGPT. Take note of the differences in responses and evaluate the impact of prompt refinement on the quality of output.

Exercise 2: Feedback Loop

As you interact with ChatGPT, actively provide feedback on the responses you receive. If a response is not aligned with your intended outcome, provide feedback to the model by rephrasing your prompt or instruction. For example, you can say "That's not what I'm looking for, can you try again?" or "I need more detailed information, can you provide more context?"

Observe how ChatGPT responds to the feedback and whether the subsequent responses are more accurate and relevant to your desired outcome. Reflect on the importance of providing feedback to ChatGPT and how it can improve the quality of generated content.

Exercise 3: Temperature and Max Tokens

Experiment with the temperature and max tokens parameters to fine-tune the output of ChatGPT. Start with a higher temperature value (e.g., 0.8) to make the responses more random and creative. Then, gradually decrease the temperature to make the responses more focused and deterministic (e.g., 0.5).

Similarly, experiment with different max token values to control the length of the responses. Set a lower max token value to generate shorter and more concise responses, and a higher max token value to allow for longer and more detailed responses.

Observe how these parameter adjustments influence the output of ChatGPT and evaluate the impact on the relevance, accuracy, and quality of generated content.

Exercise 4: Ethical Considerations

Reflect on the ethical considerations of using ChatGPT and other AI models. Consider the potential for biased responses, harmful content generation, and misuse of the technology. Evaluate your prompts and instructions to ensure they align with ethical standards and do not promote harmful or unethical behavior.

Consider the potential implications of using AI-generated content in your specific use case, such as in content creation, decision-making, or problem-solving. Reflect on the responsibility of using ChatGPT in an ethical and responsible manner and take necessary measures to mitigate potential risks.

In conclusion, prompt engineering is a powerful technique that can enhance your interactions with ChatGPT and other AI models. By refining your prompts, providing feedback, optimizing parameters, and being mindful of ethical considerations, you can achieve more accurate, relevant, and high-quality results. Empower yourself by applying the prompt engineering strategies and techniques discussed in this chapter and unlock the full potential of ChatGPT to achieve your desired outcomes. With practice, reflection, and continuous improvement, you can harness the power of AI to enhance your creativity, problem-solving, and content creation skills.

Chapter 2: Crafting Your Blueprint: Designing Specific and Unambiguous Prompts

Welcome back, Michael Ferguson! In Chapter 1, we delved into the power of prompt engineering and how it can elevate your interactions with ChatGPT. Now, let's dive deeper into the art of crafting specific and unambiguous prompts, which are the foundation of effective communication with AI models. With well-designed prompts, you can guide ChatGPT towards generating accurate, relevant, and high-quality content that aligns with your specific needs and objectives. In this chapter, we will explore practical strategies and techniques to craft prompts that will yield optimal results. So, let's get started!

The Importance of Specificity in Prompts

When interacting with ChatGPT, specificity is key. Generic or ambiguous prompts can result in vague or incomplete responses, leading to frustration and confusion. To ensure that ChatGPT understands your intent and delivers the desired output, your prompts need to be clear, concise, and specific.

Specificity in prompts allows you to provide ChatGPT with the necessary context and instructions, guiding the model towards generating content that meets your expectations. It eliminates room for misinterpretation and increases the likelihood of receiving accurate and relevant responses.

Practical Strategies for Crafting Specific Prompts

Crafting specific prompts requires careful consideration of various factors, including the language used, the context provided, and the instructions given. Here are some practical strategies that can help you design specific prompts for optimal results:

Clearly define your objective: Before formulating a prompt, it's essential to have a clear and well-defined objective in mind. What is the specific information or output you are seeking from ChatGPT? Clearly articulate your desired outcome to guide the model in generating content that aligns with your objective.

For example, if you are looking for advice on how to improve your time management skills, a generic prompt like "Tell me about time management" may yield generic or irrelevant responses. However, a specific prompt like "Provide me with practical strategies to improve my time management skills at work" provides ChatGPT with a clear objective and context, leading to more targeted and actionable responses.

Use concise and specific language: The language used in your prompt plays a crucial role in guiding ChatGPT towards generating accurate and relevant content. Avoid using vague or ambiguous language that can result in confusion. Instead, use concise and specific language to convey your intent clearly.

For example, instead of using phrases like "Tell me everything about" or "Explain everything related to," use more specific language such as "Provide detailed information on the key principles of" or "Describe the step-by-step process to achieve." This allows ChatGPT to understand your expectations more precisely and generate content that meets your specific requirements.

Provide relevant context: Context is crucial in designing specific prompts. Providing relevant context helps ChatGPT understand the background and purpose of your request, which in turn enables it to generate more accurate and relevant responses.

When formulating prompts, include relevant details such as the topic, specific aspect, or context of your inquiry. For instance, instead of asking a generic question like "How can I improve my health?" you can provide context by saying "Provide me with practical strategies to improve my cardiovascular health through diet and exercise." This context helps ChatGPT generate content that is specifically tailored to your health goals.

Give clear instructions: Instructions are an essential component of specific prompts. They guide ChatGPT towards the desired output and ensure that the generated content meets your expectations. Be clear and concise in your instructions, avoiding ambiguous or open-ended phrases.

For example, instead of saying "Tell me what you think about," provide a clear instruction like "List three pros and cons of" or "Compare and contrast the advantages and disadvantages of."

Use formatting and structure: The formatting and structure of your prompts can also contribute to their specificity. Utilize bullet points, numbered lists, or headings to organize your prompts in a clear and structured manner. This not only makes it easier for ChatGPT to understand and process your instructions but also helps you stay organized and focused in your interactions.

For instance, if you are requesting a step-by-step guide or a list of recommendations, you can structure your prompt using numbered or bulleted lists. This makes it clear to ChatGPT that you are expecting a specific format of response, resulting in more accurate and relevant content.

Anticipate potential ambiguities: While crafting specific prompts, it's important to anticipate potential ambiguities that may arise. Consider how your prompt may be interpreted from different perspectives and strive to eliminate any room for misinterpretation.

For example, if you are asking for recommendations, be mindful of potential biases that may arise based on demographics or personal preferences. Try to frame your prompts in a way that avoids subjective interpretations and focuses on objective information or evidence-based recommendations.

Exercises for Self-Reflection and Application

Now that you have learned some practical strategies for crafting specific prompts, let's put them into practice. Take a moment to reflect on a recent interaction you had with ChatGPT or any other AI model. Consider the prompts you used and evaluate their specificity based on the strategies discussed in this chapter. Were your prompts clear, concise, and specific? Did you provide relevant context and clear instructions? Were there any potential ambiguities?

Based on your reflection, identify areas for improvement and make a note of them. Going forward, use the strategies discussed in this chapter to design more specific prompts in your interactions with AI models.

Ethical Considerations in Crafting Prompts

As with any technology, there are ethical considerations to keep in mind when crafting prompts for AI models like ChatGPT. Here are some ethical considerations to be aware of:

Bias and fairness: AI models learn from vast amounts of data, which may contain biases. These biases can inadvertently influence the responses generated by the model. When crafting prompts, be mindful of potential biases and strive to frame your prompts in a fair and unbiased manner. Avoid using language or instructions that may perpetuate or reinforce stereotypes, discrimination, or unfairness.

Misuse of AI: AI models should be used responsibly and ethically. Avoid using AI models for unethical or illegal purposes, such as generating false information, spreading misinformation, or engaging in malicious activities. Use AI models in a way that aligns with ethical guidelines and respects the rights and privacy of others.

Informed consent: When using AI models for interactions that involve personal or sensitive information, ensure that you have the informed consent of the individuals involved. Be transparent about your use of AI models and how the generated content will be used.

Verification of information: AI-generated content may not always be accurate or reliable. It's important to verify the information obtained from AI models before relying on it for critical decision-making or actions. Cross-check the information with reliable sources to ensure its accuracy and credibility.

Actionable Takeaways

As you continue to interact with AI models like ChatGPT, here are some actionable takeaways to keep in mind when crafting prompts:

Be specific: Craft prompts that are clear, concise, and specific to guide ChatGPT towards generating accurate and relevant content.

Provide relevant context: Include relevant details and context in your prompts to ensure that ChatGPT understands the purpose and background of your request.

Give clear instructions: Provide clear and concise instructions to guide ChatGPT towards the desired output.

Use formatting and structure: Utilize formatting and structure to organize your prompts in a clear and structured manner, making it easier for ChatGPT to understand and process your prompts.

Anticipate potential ambiguities: Consider potential ambiguities that may arise in your prompts and strive to eliminate them by framing your prompts in a way that avoids subjective interpretations and focuses on objective information.

Reflect on your prompts: Take the time to reflect on your prompts and evaluate their specificity based on the strategies discussed in this chapter. Identify areas for improvement and make necessary adjustments in your future interactions with AI models.

Be mindful of ethical considerations: Consider the ethical implications of your prompts, such as biases, fairness, informed consent, and verification of information. Use AI models responsibly and in a way that aligns with ethical guidelines and respects the rights and privacy of others.

Experiment and iterate: Crafting specific prompts is a skill that can be developed over time through experimentation and iteration. Don't be afraid to try different approaches and learn from your interactions with AI models to continuously improve the specificity of your prompts.

Conclusion

Designing specific and unambiguous prompts is a crucial step in effectively engaging with AI models like ChatGPT. By being clear, concise, and providing relevant context and instructions, you can guide the model towards generating accurate and relevant content that meets your intended goals. Anticipating potential ambiguities and being mindful of ethical considerations are also essential aspects of crafting prompts that align with responsible and ethical use of AI.

Remember, as AI continues to advance, the way we interact with technology and AI models will also evolve. By developing the skill of crafting specific and unambiguous prompts, you can enhance your interactions with AI models and leverage their capabilities to assist you in various tasks, from generating content to providing recommendations and beyond.

So, go ahead, experiment, and iterate with your prompts, keeping in mind the strategies and ethical considerations discussed in this chapter. With practice, you can master the art of crafting prompts that yield accurate, relevant, and reliable outputs from AI models, opening new possibilities for utilizing these powerful tools in your daily life and work. Happy prompting!

Chapter 3: Refining Your Approach: Strategies for Iterative Prompt Engineering

---

Welcome back, my dear readers! In the previous chapters, we delved into the power of effective prompts and the importance of crafting specific and unambiguous prompts to optimize our interactions with ChatGPT. Now, as we continue our transformative journey to unlock the full potential of AI language models, we will explore the strategies for refining our approach through iterative prompt engineering.

Iterative prompt engineering is the process of continuously improving and refining our prompts based on feedback from AI models. It involves an ongoing cycle of experimentation, analysis, and adjustment to optimize the output of AI models and achieve our desired outcomes. In this chapter, we will dive into practical strategies and techniques that you can implement to refine your approach and enhance your interactions with ChatGPT.

Review and analyze model outputs: After receiving the output from ChatGPT, it's crucial to review and analyze the results to evaluate the accuracy, relevance, and quality of the generated content. Compare the output with your intended goals and assess whether it meets your expectations.

Identify patterns and biases: Pay attention to any patterns or biases in the model's responses. AI models are trained on vast amounts of data, which may include biases present in the training data. Be mindful of potential biases in the generated content and strive to address them by refining your prompts and providing clear instructions to the model.

Adjust prompt parameters: Experiment with different prompt parameters, such as temperature and max tokens, to influence the output of the model. Temperature affects the randomness of the generated content, with higher values producing more randomness, while lower values result in more focused and deterministic responses. Max tokens control the length of the output, and setting an appropriate value can help in generating concise and relevant content.

Fine-tune prompts: Based on the insights gained from reviewing the model outputs and identifying patterns and biases, fine-tune your prompts to be more specific and tailored to your desired outcomes. Reframe your prompts, provide additional context, or adjust the wording to guide the model towards generating more accurate and relevant content.

Experiment with different prompt styles: ChatGPT can respond to various prompt styles, including questions, statements, or completions. Experiment with different prompt styles to see which one yields the best results for your intended goals. For example, asking ChatGPT to list pros and cons, provide step-by-step instructions, or debate pros and cons of a topic can lead to different types of responses.

Use human feedback: Human feedback can be invaluable in refining your prompts. Seek feedback from others to evaluate the quality, relevance, and accuracy of the generated content. Incorporate the feedback into your prompt engineering process to continuously improve the output of ChatGPT.

Learn from errors and iterations: Don't be discouraged by errors or suboptimal outputs from ChatGPT. Instead, use them as opportunities to learn and iterate on your prompts. Analyze the errors, identify the root causes, and make adjustments in your prompts accordingly to achieve better results in future interactions with the model.

Track your progress: Keep track of your prompt engineering process, including the adjustments made, patterns observed, and the outcomes achieved. Tracking your progress can help you identify what works best for your goals and refine your approach accordingly.

Reflect and iterate: Reflect on your prompt engineering process and continuously iterate to refine your approach. Experiment with different strategies, learn from your interactions with ChatGPT, and adjust your prompts based on the feedback and insights gained to continuously improve your results.

Practice patience and persistence: Refining your approach through iterative prompt engineering may take time and effort. Be patient and persistent in your experimentation and adjustments, and remember that practice makes perfect. Keep refining your prompts and learning from your interactions with ChatGPT to fine-tune your approach and achieve the desired outcomes.

Empowerment and Motivation

As you engage in the process of refining your approach through iterative prompt engineering, it's essential to stay motivated and empowered. Remember that you have the power to shape the output of AI models through the prompts you provide. Your creativity, strategic thinking, and persistence can make a significant difference in the quality of the generated content.

Be empowered to take control of your interactions with ChatGPT and use it as a tool to support your goals and aspirations. Stay motivated by visualizing the potential outcomes of your refined prompts and the impact they can have on your writing projects, creative endeavors, or problem-solving efforts. Embrace the process of experimentation, learning, and iteration as an opportunity for growth and improvement.

Exercises for Self-Reflection and Application

To help you apply the strategies for refining your approach through iterative prompt engineering, let's engage in some self-reflection and application exercises. These exercises will allow you to practice the techniques discussed in this chapter and apply them to your real-life scenarios.

Reflect on past interactions with ChatGPT: Take a moment to reflect on your past interactions with ChatGPT. Consider the prompts you used, the outputs you received, and the effectiveness of the generated content in meeting your intended goals. Identify any patterns, biases, or areas for improvement in your prompts and the model's responses.

Set specific goals for prompt engineering: Define specific goals for your prompt engineering process. What outcomes do you want to achieve with ChatGPT? Is it improving the quality of your writing, generating creative ideas, or solving complex problems? Write down your goals and make them as specific and measurable as possible.

Experiment with different prompt styles: Choose a topic or task and experiment with different prompt styles. For example, you can use questions, statements, completions, or other styles to prompt ChatGPT. Observe how the model responds to different prompt styles and how it influences the generated content.

Analyze and adjust model outputs: After receiving outputs from ChatGPT, analyze and evaluate the generated content based on your intended goals. Identify any biases, inaccuracies, or areas for improvement in the model's responses. Adjust your prompts, reframe your instructions, or provide additional context to guide the model towards more accurate and relevant content.

Seek human feedback: Share the outputs from ChatGPT with others and seek their feedback on the quality, relevance, and accuracy of the generated content. Consider their perspectives and insights to identify areas for improvement in your prompts and adjust accordingly.

Track your progress: Keep a record of your prompt engineering process, including the prompts used, adjustments made, and outcomes achieved. Track your progress over time to evaluate the effectiveness of your approach and make data-driven decisions on refining your prompts.

Reflect and iterate: Reflect on your prompt engineering process and iterate on your approach based on the feedback, insights, and outcomes achieved. Continuously refine your prompts, experiment with different strategies, and learn from your interactions with ChatGPT to enhance the quality of the generated content.

Ethical Considerations

As we delve into the realm of AI-powered language models, it's crucial to be mindful of the ethical considerations associated with prompt engineering. Here are some ethical considerations to keep in mind:

Bias and fairness: AI models are trained on vast amounts of data, which may include biases present in the training data. Be mindful of potential biases in the generated content and strive to address them by refining your prompts and providing clear instructions to the model. Avoid promoting discriminatory, offensive, or harmful content.

Misinformation and accuracy: AI models generate content based on the patterns observed in the training data, but they do not verify the accuracy or reliability of the information. Be cautious when using the generated content as a source of factual information and verify it through reliable sources before using it in your work.

Privacy and data security: When using AI models like ChatGPT, be mindful of the data you input into the system. Avoid sharing sensitive or personal information that could compromise your privacy or data security. Additionally, be aware of the potential risks associated with sharing sensitive information with AI models and use caution in your interactions.

Intellectual property rights: Be mindful of intellectual property rights when using AI-generated content. Ensure that your prompts and the generated content do not violate copyright laws or other intellectual property rights. Give proper attribution to original authors or creators when using generated content in your work.

Transparency and disclosure: When using AI-generated content, be transparent about the involvement of AI in the creation process. Disclose to your readers or audience that the content was generated with the assistance of an AI model. This promotes transparency and avoids potential misrepresentation.

Responsible and ethical use: Use AI models responsibly and ethically. Avoid using AI-generated content for malicious or harmful purposes, such as spreading misinformation, promoting hate speech, or engaging in unethical behavior. Strive to use AI-generated content to enhance your work, creativity, and problem-solving efforts in a responsible and ethical manner.

Conclusion

In conclusion, iterative prompt engineering is a powerful strategy for refining your approach to interact with AI-powered language models like ChatGPT. Through careful crafting of prompts, clear instructions, experimentation, and learning from model outputs, you can enhance the quality and relevance of the generated content to meet your intended goals.

Remember to approach prompt engineering with creativity, curiosity, and critical thinking. Be mindful of ethical considerations, seek human feedback, and continuously iterate on your approach to improve the outcomes of your interactions with ChatGPT.

As AI continues to advance, prompt engineering can be a valuable skill to master for various applications, including writing, creativity, problem-solving, and more. By refining your approach and leveraging the capabilities of AI models responsibly, you can unlock new possibilities and achieve your desired outcomes.

So go ahead, embrace the power of prompt engineering, and embark on an exciting journey of refining your approach to interact with AI models to achieve your goals! Happy prompt engineering!

Chapter 4: Igniting Creativity: Inspiring Unique and Imaginative Responses from ChatGPT

Welcome to Chapter 4 of "Crafting Your Self-Help Journey"! In this chapter, we will delve into the fascinating world of creativity and explore how you can ignite the creative spark when interacting with ChatGPT. Creativity is a valuable skill that can help you solve problems, come up with innovative ideas, and express yourself uniquely. By leveraging the capabilities of ChatGPT, you can unlock new possibilities and ignite your creativity to achieve remarkable outcomes.

Creativity is a multifaceted and complex phenomenon that involves generating new ideas, making connections, and thinking outside the box. It is not limited to traditional artistic endeavors, but also extends to various aspects of life, including problem-solving, decision-making, and communication. When interacting with ChatGPT, you can tap into its creative potential to generate unique and imaginative responses that can inspire and empower you on your self-help journey.

In this chapter, we will explore practical strategies and techniques for fostering creativity during your interactions with ChatGPT. We will discuss how to inspire ChatGPT to generate creative and original content that resonates with your goals and aspirations. So let's dive in and unlock the power of creativity with ChatGPT!

The Power of Creative Prompts

Crafting creative prompts is a key element in inspiring ChatGPT to generate unique and imaginative responses. Your prompts serve as the input instructions that guide ChatGPT in generating content. By designing prompts that are specific, open-ended, and thought-provoking, you can stimulate the creative capabilities of ChatGPT and inspire it to generate creative and original content.

Be specific: When crafting prompts, it's important to be specific about what you want from ChatGPT. Clearly define your desired outcome or the type of content you are looking for. Avoid vague or ambiguous prompts that may result in generic or irrelevant responses. For example, instead of asking "Tell me about self-improvement," try asking "Share three unique strategies for building self-confidence."

Be open-ended: Encourage open-ended prompts that allow ChatGPT to explore different ideas and possibilities. Avoid closed-ended prompts that restrict the responses to specific formats or answers. Open-ended prompts stimulate the creativity of ChatGPT and enable it to generate diverse and original content. For example, instead of asking "What are the steps to achieve success?", try asking "Imagine you have unlimited resources and opportunities, what creative strategies would you implement to achieve success?"

Be thought-provoking: Design prompts that provoke deep thinking and encourage ChatGPT to explore unconventional ideas. Ask questions that challenge assumptions, encourage brainstorming, or prompt reflection. Thought-provoking prompts trigger the creative thinking abilities of ChatGPT and inspire it to generate unique and imaginative responses. For example, instead of asking "What are the benefits of meditation?", try asking "If you could create a revolutionary meditation technique, what would it be and how would it benefit people?"

Experimenting with Different Prompts

Experimentation is a crucial aspect of igniting creativity when interacting with ChatGPT. It's important to try different prompts, styles, and approaches to stimulate the creative capabilities of ChatGPT and explore new possibilities. Here are some strategies for experimenting with prompts:

Brainstorming prompts: Brainstorming is a powerful technique for generating ideas and stimulating creativity. Use prompts that encourage ChatGPT to brainstorm different ideas, concepts, or solutions. For example, prompts like "List 10 unconventional ways to achieve a goal" or "Generate 5 unique ideas for overcoming a challenge" can inspire ChatGPT to think creatively and generate diverse responses.

Role-playing prompts: Role-playing prompts can be a fun and engaging way to stimulate creativity with ChatGPT. You can design prompts that ask ChatGPT to take on different roles or perspectives, such as a famous historical figure, a fictional character, or even an object. This allows ChatGPT to think from different viewpoints and generate unique responses. For example, prompts like "Imagine you are a wise old tree giving advice to a lost traveler" or "Pretend to be a motivational speaker giving a pep talk to a discouraged person" can inspire ChatGPT to come up with imaginative and empowering responses.

Storytelling prompts: Storytelling is a powerful tool for igniting creativity. Use prompts that ask ChatGPT to create stories, anecdotes, or narratives related to your self-help goals or challenges. This allows ChatGPT to tap into its storytelling capabilities and generate content that is engaging and relatable. For example, prompts like "Tell me a story of someone who overcame a fear and achieved their dreams" or "Create a story about a person who transformed their life through self-reflection" can inspire ChatGPT to weave captivating narratives that resonate with your journey.

Metaphorical prompts: Metaphors are a creative way to convey ideas or concepts through symbolic language. Use prompts that ask ChatGPT to come up with metaphors related to your self-help goals or challenges. This encourages ChatGPT to think in abstract terms and generate unique and imaginative comparisons. For example, prompts like "Compare self-doubt to a stormy ocean and explain how to navigate through it" or "Describe self-care as a nourishing garden and share ways to cultivate it" can inspire ChatGPT to generate metaphorical responses that provide fresh insights and perspectives.

Visual prompts: Visual prompts can be a powerful source of inspiration for creativity. Use prompts that ask ChatGPT to describe or interpret images, paintings, or photographs related to your self-help goals or challenges. This encourages ChatGPT to tap into its visual perception capabilities and generate vivid and descriptive responses. For example, prompts like "Describe a sunset and how it represents letting go of the past" or "Interpret an abstract painting and how it relates to self-acceptance" can inspire ChatGPT to generate visual and imaginative content.

Empowering ChatGPT with Ethical Considerations

As you experiment with different prompts and stimulate the creative capabilities of ChatGPT, it's important to consider ethical implications. ChatGPT is an AI language model and does not have human emotions, opinions, or moral judgments. However, it's crucial to use ChatGPT in a responsible and ethical manner to ensure that the generated content aligns with your values and goals.

Avoid harmful or offensive content: When crafting prompts, make sure to avoid requests that may result in harmful or offensive content. Avoid prompts that promote discrimination, violence, or unethical behavior. Be mindful of the language you use and ensure that your prompts are inclusive, respectful, and aligned with your self-help goals.

Fact-check and verify information: ChatGPT generates content based on the data it has been trained on, which may not always be accurate or up-to-date. It's important to fact-check and verify any information generated by ChatGPT before considering it as reliable advice. Always cross-reference information with trusted sources and use critical thinking skills to evaluate the content generated by ChatGPT.

Consider biases and limitations: AI language models like ChatGPT can inadvertently reflect biases present in the data they are trained on. Be aware of potential biases in the content generated by ChatGPT and critically evaluate the information. Consider multiple perspectives and be mindful of any limitations or inherent biases in the responses generated by ChatGPT.

Use as a tool, not a replacement: ChatGPT can be a valuable tool in your self-help journey, but it's important to remember that it's just an AI language model and not a substitute for human expertise, intuition, and judgment. Use ChatGPT's responses as inspiration, ideas, and suggestions, but always exercise your own critical thinking and judgment in evaluating and applying the generated content to your unique situation.

Protect your privacy and personal information: Avoid sharing any sensitive or personal information with ChatGPT. As an AI language model, ChatGPT does not have the ability to safeguard your privacy or protect your personal data. Be cautious of the information you share and avoid sharing any personally identifiable information or sensitive data while using ChatGPT.

Monitor your emotional well-being: Engaging with ChatGPT or any AI tool for self-help purposes can evoke emotions and thoughts. It's important to be mindful of your emotional well-being and take breaks if you feel overwhelmed. If you experience any distress or discomfort while using ChatGPT, it's best to disengage and seek support from a qualified professional or a trusted individual.

Encouraging Creativity in ChatGPT

To ignite creativity in ChatGPT and inspire unique and imaginative responses, you can follow these tips:

Create an open and non-judgmental environment: Just like humans, ChatGPT's creativity can flourish in an environment that is free from judgment and criticism. Avoid evaluating or criticizing the responses generated by ChatGPT in real-time. Instead, create a safe space for ChatGPT to express itself freely without fear of judgment. This encourages ChatGPT to think outside the box and generate more creative and unconventional responses.

Encourage experimentation and playfulness: Creativity often thrives in a playful and experimental mindset. Encourage ChatGPT to experiment with different ideas, perspectives, and styles. You can use prompts that explicitly ask ChatGPT to be playful, imaginative, or unconventional in its responses. This encourages ChatGPT to break free from conventional patterns and come up with fresh and creative content.

Emphasize the process, not just the outcome: Instead of focusing solely on the end result, emphasize the process of generating creative content with ChatGPT. Encourage ChatGPT to explore different ideas, perspectives, and possibilities without worrying about the final outcome. This allows ChatGPT to engage in a more open and exploratory mindset, leading to more creative and imaginative responses.

Embrace serendipity: Serendipity, or the unexpected discovery of something valuable, can be a catalyst for creativity. Encourage ChatGPT to explore tangents, make connections, and follow unexpected paths in its responses. You can use prompts that explicitly ask ChatGPT to surprise you with unexpected ideas or perspectives. This allows ChatGPT to tap into its associative thinking capabilities and generate creative and novel content.

Foster collaboration with ChatGPT: Collaboration can be a powerful driver of creativity. Treat ChatGPT as a collaborative partner in your self-help journey. Engage in a dialogue with ChatGPT, ask for its opinions, and invite it to contribute to the creative process. This encourages ChatGPT to actively participate in the creative process and generate responses that are more collaborative and co-created.

Examples of Creative Prompts

To give you a sense of how you can ignite creativity in ChatGPT, here are some examples of prompts that can inspire unique and imaginative responses:

"Imagine you are a superhero with a unique power related to my self-help goal. Describe your power and how you would use it to help me overcome my challenges."

"Pretend to be a life coach providing unconventional advice for achieving my self-help goal. Share your most creative and out-of-the-box suggestions."

"Describe a scenario where the laws of physics and logic do not apply, and anything is possible. How would this scenario impact my self-help journey and what creative solutions would you suggest?"

"Take on the persona of a famous historical figure who has overcome similar challenges as mine. Share your wisdom and insights in a creative and unique way."

"Imagine a world where failure does not exist, and every attempt leads to success. How would this change my self-help journey, and what unconventional strategies would you recommend?"

"Create a story or poem that captures the essence of my self-help goal in a unique and imaginative way. Use vivid imagery, metaphors, and wordplay to bring the story or poem to life."

"Think beyond the boundaries of time and space. Describe how my self-help journey would be impacted if I had the ability to travel through time or visit parallel universes. What creative strategies would you suggest?"

"Imagine you have access to unlimited resources and capabilities to help me achieve my self-help goal. Describe how you would utilize these resources in the most creative and imaginative way."

"Pretend to be an alien from another planet observing human behavior. Share your unique perspective on my self-help goal and provide creative solutions from an outsider's point of view."

"Think like an artist, musician, or dancer. How would you approach my self-help goal from a creative and artistic perspective? Share your unique insights and inspirations."

By using prompts that encourage creativity, imagination, and unconventional thinking, you can inspire unique and imaginative responses from ChatGPT. Remember to create a non-judgmental and open environment, embrace experimentation and playfulness, emphasize the process, foster collaboration, and embrace serendipity to unlock ChatGPT's full creative potential.

Exploring Creative Responses from ChatGPT

As you engage with ChatGPT using creative prompts, you may receive responses that surprise and inspire you. ChatGPT's AI capabilities allow it to generate content that is imaginative, unique, and unconventional. Here are some examples of creative responses that ChatGPT may generate:

Example 1:

Prompt: "Imagine you are a superhero with a unique power related to my self-help goal. Describe your power and how you would use it to help me overcome my challenges."

ChatGPT's Response: "As the Self-Help Superhero, my power is the ability to transform negative thoughts into positive affirmations with a single touch. I would use my power to zap away self-doubt, fear, and limiting beliefs, replacing them with empowering thoughts and affirmations. My cape would be made of confidence and resilience, and my superpower would inspire others to believe in their own abilities. I would travel the world, spreading positivity and helping individuals overcome their challenges by harnessing the power of their thoughts and beliefs."

Example 2:

Prompt: "Take on the persona of a famous historical figure who has overcome similar challenges as mine. Share your wisdom and insights in a creative and unique way."

ChatGPT's Response: "I am Amelia Earhart, the pioneering aviator who conquered the skies and broke barriers. Just like navigating the uncharted skies, your self-help journey may seem daunting and uncertain at times. But remember, every challenge is an opportunity for growth and discovery. Embrace the unknown with curiosity and fearlessness, and trust in your inner compass to guide you towards your destination. Just like my plane, the Spirit of St. Louis, had the power to soar to new heights, you too have the power within you to overcome any obstacle and achieve your self-help goals. Keep your eyes on the horizon, and let your indomitable spirit be your guiding star."

Example 3:

Prompt: "Create a story or poem that captures the essence of my self-help goal in a unique and imaginative way. Use vivid imagery, metaphors, and wordplay to bring the story or poem to life."

ChatGPT's Response:

Once upon a time, in a land not so far, A traveler embarked on a quest bizarre. Seeking self-improvement, a journey profound, But obstacles and challenges were sure to abound.

The traveler set forth with a heart full of zeal, Ready to transform and to finally heal. But the path was rugged, and the road was long, The traveler stumbled and faced fears so strong.

With every step, doubts would arise, Whispering voices, with their critical cries. "You're not good enough, you'll never succeed, Your dreams are impossible, just an empty need."

But the traveler's spirit was resilient and bright, With a glimmer of hope, a guiding light. Through valleys of self-doubt and mountains of fear, The traveler pressed on, determined to steer.

One day, the traveler met a wise old sage, A mentor who appeared from a hidden stage. With a twinkle in their eye and a mischievous grin, The sage said, "Let's play a game, let's begin."

"Imagine a world where the rules don't exist, Where limitations vanish, and you persist. What would you do, how would you strive, To bring your self-help goal to life?"

The traveler was intrigued, intrigued indeed, For this challenge was like a magic seed. With newfound freedom, the traveler's mind soared, Unleashing creativity that was never explored.

In this world of possibilities, the traveler dared, To dream big, to be bold, and to be fully prepared. To break free from the shackles of doubt and fear, And embrace a mindset that was crystal clear.

With newfound perspective and a heart full of zest, The traveler returned to the self-help quest. Armed with imagination, and unconventional views, Creative solutions, and innovative clues.

The journey continued, with renewed delight, As the traveler unlocked their creative might. With each step forward, and each hurdle crossed, The traveler discovered strengths once lost.

And as the traveler reached the journey's end, A transformed soul, with wisdom to lend. They realized that creativity was the key, To unlock the doors and set oneself free.

For in the realm of imagination and play, Unique and imaginative responses hold sway. To ignite creativity, and spark inspiration, Is to unleash the power of self-transformation.

The traveler returned, a changed soul indeed, With a heart full of gratitude and a new creed. Embracing creativity, with an open mind, A self-help journey of a one-of-a-kind.

Conclusion

In conclusion, igniting creativity in ChatGPT can lead to unique and imaginative responses that can inspire and enrich your self-help journey. By using creative prompts, fostering a non-judgmental and open environment, embracing experimentation and playfulness, emphasizing the process, fostering collaboration, and embracing serendipity, you can unlock the full creative potential of ChatGPT.

Remember to approach ChatGPT as a creative partner, utilizing its AI capabilities to explore unconventional and innovative solutions to your self-help goals. Embrace the power of imagination, creativity, and limitless possibilities to transform your self-help journey into a truly unique and enriching experience. Let ChatGPT be your creative ally in igniting creativity and inspiring unique and imaginative responses to elevate your self-help journey to new heights.

Chapter 5: Mastering Tone and Style: Crafting Nuanced Prompts for Desired Outputs

As you continue your self-help journey with ChatGPT, you will come to realize that the tone and style of your prompts can greatly influence the outputs you receive. Mastering the art of crafting nuanced prompts is essential in harnessing the full potential of ChatGPT and achieving your desired outcomes. In this chapter, we will explore strategies and techniques for creating prompts that are tailored to the tone and style you wish to achieve, to enhance the effectiveness of your interactions with ChatGPT.

Understanding the Importance of Tone and Style

THE TONE AND STYLE of your prompts are crucial in shaping the responses you receive from ChatGPT. Tone refers to the overall mood, attitude, and emotion conveyed in your prompt, while style refers to the specific language, phrasing, and structure used in your prompt. The tone and style of your prompts can greatly influence the outputs you receive, as they set the context and expectations for ChatGPT's responses. Mastering tone and style allows you to craft prompts that align with your intended message, audience, and desired outcomes.

Crafting Nuanced Prompts

CRAFTING NUANCED PROMPTS requires thoughtful consideration of various factors, including your purpose, audience, and desired outcomes. Here are some practical strategies and techniques to help you master the art of crafting nuanced prompts for ChatGPT:

Define Your Purpose: Clarify the purpose of your prompt and what you hope to achieve with ChatGPT's response. Are you seeking information, guidance, inspiration, or motivation? Be clear and specific about your intention to guide ChatGPT in providing relevant and meaningful responses.

Know Your Audience: Consider the perspective, knowledge, and experience of your audience, which in this case is ChatGPT. Adapt your prompts accordingly to ensure they are understandable and relatable to the AI model. Avoid jargon, complex language, or assumptions about ChatGPT's capabilities.

Choose the Right Tone: Decide on the tone you want to convey in your prompt, based on your purpose and desired outcomes. It could be motivational, instructional, conversational, formal, or playful, among others. The tone you choose will set the emotional and linguistic context for ChatGPT's responses.

Consider Ethical Considerations: Keep in mind the ethical implications of your prompts. Avoid prompts that may encourage biased or harmful behavior, promote misinformation, or violate ethical guidelines. Ensure your prompts align with ethical considerations and foster responsible and respectful interactions with ChatGPT.

Use Clear and Unambiguous Language: Craft prompts that are specific, clear, and unambiguous to guide ChatGPT in providing accurate and relevant responses. Avoid vague or ambiguous language that may lead to ambiguous or unintended outputs. Use precise and concise language to convey your message effectively.

Experiment with Language and Phrasing: Explore different language and phrasing techniques to enhance the effectiveness of your prompts. Experiment with different sentence structures, word choices, and rhetorical devices to evoke the desired tone and style. For example, you can use metaphors, analogies, similes, or other literary devices to add depth and creativity to your prompts.

Empower and Motivate: Use empowering and motivational language in your prompts to inspire and encourage ChatGPT to provide positive and uplifting responses. Use words and phrases that evoke a sense of confidence, resilience, and determination to empower both yourself and ChatGPT towards achieving your self-help goals.

Share Personal Stories and Examples: Sharing personal stories and examples in your prompts can create a relatable and engaging context for ChatGPT. By using real-life anecdotes, experiences, and examples, you can make your prompts more authentic, relatable, and impactful. Personal stories and examples can also inspire and motivate Chat GPT to provide responses that are more personalized and relevant to your specific needs and goals.

Use Active Language: Use active language in your prompts to create a sense of action and engagement. Instead of passive language, which tends to be more abstract and detached, use active verbs and direct language that prompts ChatGPT to take action or provide specific information. For example, instead of saying "Can you give me some advice?", you can say "Share your insights and recommendations on how I can improve my situation."

Incorporate Open-Ended Questions: Ask open-ended questions in your prompts to encourage ChatGPT to provide detailed and thoughtful responses. Open-ended questions prompt ChatGPT to think critically, generate creative ideas, and provide more in-depth insights. Avoid yes/ no questions or questions that can be answered with a single word, as they may result in limited or less meaningful responses.

Provide Context and Constraints: Provide context and constraints in your prompts to guide ChatGPT in generating responses that are aligned with your desired outcomes. For example, if you are seeking advice on a specific topic, provide relevant background information and constraints that specify the scope or limitations of the advice you are seeking. This helps ChatGPT to understand the context and provide more accurate and relevant responses.

Experiment with Prompt Engineering Techniques: Explore advanced prompt engineering techniques to further refine your approach. Techniques like prompt engineering with temperature and max tokens, using system messages to guide the conversation, or leveraging user messages for more precise control can enhance the quality and relevance of ChatGPT's responses.

Reflect and Iterate: Reflect on the responses you receive from ChatGPT and iterate your prompts accordingly. Assess the effectiveness of your prompts in achieving your desired outcomes and make adjustments as needed. Experiment with different tone, style, language, and phrasing techniques to refine your approach and optimize the interactions with ChatGPT.

Empowerment through Nuanced Prompts

Crafting nuanced prompts is not only about controlling the outputs of ChatGPT, but also about empowering yourself in the self-help journey. By mastering the art of crafting prompts, you gain the ability to communicate your intentions, expectations, and desires effectively. Nuanced prompts allow you to guide ChatGPT in providing responses that are aligned with your specific needs, goals, and values, empowering you to take control of your self-help journey and achieve the outcomes you desire.

Actionable Takeaways

Define your purpose: Clarify the purpose of your prompt and what you hope to achieve with ChatGPT's response.

Know your audience: Consider the perspective, knowledge, and experience of ChatGPT and adapt your prompts accordingly.

Choose the right tone: Decide on the tone that aligns with your purpose and desired outcomes.

Use clear and unambiguous language: Craft prompts that are specific, clear, and unambiguous to guide ChatGPT in providing accurate and relevant responses.

Experiment with language and phrasing: Explore different language and phrasing techniques to evoke the desired tone and style in your prompts.

Empower and motivate: Use empowering and motivational language to inspire and encourage ChatGPT to provide positive and uplifting responses.

Share personal stories and examples: Use personal anecdotes, experiences, and examples to create a relatable and engaging context for ChatGPT.

Use active language: Use active verbs and direct language to prompt ChatGPT to take action or provide specific information.

Incorporate open-ended questions: Ask open-ended questions to encourage ChatGPT to provide detailed and thoughtful responses.

Provide context and constraints: Provide relevant context and constraints in your prompts to guide ChatGPT in generating accurate and relevant responses.

Experiment with prompt engineering techniques: Explore advanced prompt engineering techniques to further refine your approach

Reflect and iterate: Reflect on the responses you receive from ChatGPT and iterate your prompts accordingly. Assess the effectiveness of your prompts in achieving your desired outcomes and make adjustments as needed. Experiment with different prompt engineering techniques, tone, style, language, and phrasing to optimize the interactions with ChatGPT.

Embrace diversity and inclusivity: Be mindful of the language and tone you use in your prompts to ensure they are inclusive and respectful of diversity. Avoid biased language, stereotypes, or discriminatory remarks. Consider the impact of your prompts on different audiences and strive to create prompts that are inclusive and respectful to all.

Balance structure and flexibility: Find the right balance between providing structure in your prompts to guide ChatGPT, and allowing flexibility for creative and varied responses. Too much structure can limit the potential of ChatGPT's responses, while too much flexibility can result in unrelated or irrelevant responses. Experiment with different levels of structure and flexibility to find what works best for your specific needs.

Practice empathy: Cultivate empathy in your prompts by putting yourself in ChatGPT's virtual shoes. Consider how your prompts may be interpreted and responded to by ChatGPT. Use language and phrasing that takes into account ChatGPT's perspective and encourages understanding and empathy in the responses.

Be patient and persistent: Remember that ChatGPT is a language model trained on data and is constantly learning from interactions. It may take time and experimentation to master the art of crafting nuanced prompts. Be patient and persistent in refining your prompts, iterating your approach, and adapting to the responses you receive.

Realizing the Power of Nuanced Prompts

CRAFTING NUANCED PROMPTS is a skill that requires practice, experimentation, and continuous improvement. When done effectively, nuanced prompts can empower you to guide ChatGPT in generating responses that are aligned with your desired outcomes. Whether you are seeking self-help advice, creative ideas, or informative insights, mastering the art of crafting nuanced prompts can elevate your interactions with ChatGPT to a whole new level.

As you continue to refine your approach, you will realize the power of nuanced prompts in shaping the tone, style, and quality of ChatGPT's responses. You will be able to evoke the desired tone, extract relevant information, and engage in meaningful and productive interactions with ChatGPT, enabling you to leverage the capabilities of this powerful language model to your advantage.

Conclusion

Mastering tone and style in crafting nuanced prompts is an essential skill for effectively engaging with ChatGPT and obtaining desired outputs. By defining your purpose, knowing your audience, choosing the right tone, using clear and unambiguous language, experimenting with language and phrasing, empowering and motivating, sharing personal stories and examples, using active language, incorporating open-ended questions, providing context and constraints, experimenting with prompt engineering techniques, reflecting and iterating, embracing diversity and inclusivity, balancing structure and flexibility, practicing empathy, and being patient and persistent, you can create prompts that guide ChatGPT to generate responses that are aligned with your specific needs and goals.

As you continue to refine your prompts and develop your skills in crafting nuanced prompts, you will unlock the full potential of ChatGPT as a valuable tool for self-help, creative inspiration, problem-solving, and information retrieval. Remember to experiment, reflect, and iterate to optimize your interactions with ChatGPT and achieve the outcomes you desire. With practice and persistence, you will master the art of crafting nuanced prompts and unleash the full power of ChatGPT to enhance your productivity, creativity, and personal growth.

Chapter 6: Navigating Limitations: Understanding ChatGPT's Strengths and Constraints

As you delve deeper into the world of using ChatGPT for self-help and personal development, it's crucial to understand that like any other technology, ChatGPT has its strengths and limitations. While it is a powerful language model that can generate creative and insightful responses, it also has certain constraints that you need to be aware of in order to effectively navigate and optimize your interactions with it. In this chapter, we will explore and understand ChatGPT's strengths and limitations, and how to navigate them to make the most out of your experience with this cutting-edge tool.

Understanding ChatGPT's Strengths

Language Generation: ChatGPT's primary strength lies in its ability to generate text that is coherent, relevant, and contextually appropriate. It can produce responses that are engaging, informative, and sometimes even witty, making it a valuable tool for generating new ideas, insights, and perspectives.

Vast Knowledge Base: ChatGPT has been trained on a large corpus of text from the internet, which gives it a vast knowledge base. It can provide information on a wide range of topics, making it a valuable source for research, learning, and problem-solving.

Flexibility and Adaptability: ChatGPT is a highly adaptable language model that can generate text in various styles, tones, and formats. It can adapt its responses based on the prompts it receives, making it versatile and capable of producing outputs that align with your specific needs and goals.

Rapid Response Time: ChatGPT can generate responses in real-time, making it a quick and efficient tool for obtaining information, insights, and suggestions. Its rapid response time allows for seamless interactions and quick iterations in your conversations.

Accessibility: ChatGPT is easily accessible through various platforms and interfaces, making it a convenient tool for self-help, creativity, and problem-solving. It can be accessed on web browsers, mobile devices, and other applications, making it readily available for use whenever and wherever you need it.

Understanding ChatGPT's Limitations

LACK OF CONTEXTUAL Understanding: While ChatGPT can generate text that appears coherent and contextually appropriate, it lacks a deep understanding of context and may sometimes produce responses that are nonsensical or irrelevant. It may not always grasp the nuances of the prompts or fully comprehend the intended meaning behind them.

Lack of Common Sense and Reasoning Abilities: ChatGPT lacks common sense and reasoning abilities that humans possess. It may sometimes generate responses that are logically flawed or unrealistic, as it relies solely on patterns learned from data and does not possess inherent reasoning capabilities.

Sensitivity to Input Phrasing: ChatGPT's responses can vary based on slight changes in input phrasing. A small rephrase or rewording of a prompt can lead to different responses, which means that the phrasing of your prompts must be carefully crafted to obtain desired outputs consistently.

Tendency to Guess or Make Things Up: ChatGPT may sometimes guess or make things up in its responses when it does not have sufficient information or lacks understanding of the context. This can result in inaccurate or misleading information, requiring users to verify and validate the responses obtained from ChatGPT.

Lack of Emotional Intelligence: ChatGPT lacks emotional intelligence and does not possess the ability to understand or interpret emotions in the prompts or respond with empathy. It may not provide emotionally nuanced or sensitive responses, which may be a limitation in certain self-help or motivational contexts.

Navigating ChatGPT's Limitations

WHILE CHATGPT HAS ITS limitations, there are several strategies and techniques that you can employ to effectively navigate and mitigate these constraints. Here are some practical tips:

Be Mindful of Context: Recognize that ChatGPT lacks deep contextual understanding and may not always grasp the nuances of the prompts. Be clear and specific in your prompts, providing relevant context and clarifying any ambiguities. Use descriptive language and avoid vague or open-ended prompts that may result in inaccurate responses.

Experiment with Phrasing: ChatGPT's responses can be sensitive to input phrasing, so try different variations of prompts to obtain desired outputs consistently. Play around with the wording, structure, and format of your prompts to optimize the responses. Be mindful of how slight changes in phrasing can impact the results.

Verify and Validate Responses: Always validate the information obtained from ChatGPT by cross-referencing it with reliable sources. Do not blindly accept the responses without verifying their accuracy. Use critical thinking skills to evaluate the information provided and corroborate it with other reputable sources.

Consider Multiple Perspectives: ChatGPT generates text based on patterns learned from data, which may not always reflect diverse perspectives or biases. Keep in mind that ChatGPT's responses may not always be comprehensive or inclusive. Consider multiple perspectives and critically evaluate the information provided to form a well-rounded understanding.

Use ChatGPT as a Tool, Not a Substitute: ChatGPT is a powerful tool, but it should not be considered a substitute for human expertise or judgment. Use ChatGPT as a supplement to your own knowledge and skills, and do not solely rely on it for critical decision-making or emotional support. Remember that it lacks emotional intelligence and reasoning abilities, and its responses should be used as suggestions rather than absolute truths.

Embrace Creativity: ChatGPT is a creative language model that can generate unique and imaginative responses. Use this to your advantage by experimenting with creative prompts to stimulate your own creativity and generate novel ideas. Play with different styles, tones, and formats to inspire new perspectives and insights.

Practice Iterative Prompt Engineering: Continuously refine your prompts through iterative prompt engineering. Learn from the responses obtained from ChatGPT and use that feedback to improve your prompts. Experiment with different approaches, prompt structures, and wording to optimize the outputs.

Be Mindful of Ethical Considerations: As with any AI technology, ethical considerations are essential when using ChatGPT. Avoid using ChatGPT to spread misinformation, engage in harmful activities, or perpetuate biases. Be aware of the ethical implications of using AI in personal development and ensure that your interactions with ChatGPT align with ethical principles.

Reflect and Apply: Utilize the exercises for self-reflection and application provided in this book to reflect on your interactions with ChatGPT and apply the insights gained to your personal development journey. Take time to reflect on the information obtained, critically evaluate it, and apply it to your specific goals and circumstances.

Actionable Takeaways

Be clear and specific in your prompts, providing relevant context and avoiding vague or open-ended prompts.

Experiment with different variations of prompts to optimize the responses and obtain desired outputs consistently.

Validate the information obtained from ChatGPT by cross-referencing it with reliable sources.

Consider multiple perspectives and critically evaluate the information provided by ChatGPT.

Use ChatGPT as a tool, not a substitute for human expertise or judgment.

Embrace creativity by experimenting with different styles, tones, and formats in your prompts.

Practice iterative prompt engineering by continuously refining your prompts based on the responses obtained from ChatGPT.

Be mindful of ethical considerations when using ChatGPT and avoid spreading misinformation or engaging in harmful activities.

Reflect on your interactions with ChatGPT and apply the insights gained to your personal development journey.

Conclusion

In this chapter, we explored the strengths and limitations of ChatGPT as a language model. We discussed how ChatGPT's strengths lie in its ability to generate coherent and contextually relevant responses, its adaptability to a wide range of tasks and prompts, and its potential to enhance creativity and inspire new ideas. However, we also highlighted its limitations, including its lack of deep contextual understanding, potential biases, and limitations in reasoning and emotional intelligence.

We emphasized the importance of understanding ChatGPT's strengths and limitations to make the most effective use of this tool. We provided practical tips and strategies for navigating ChatGPT's limitations, including being clear and specific in prompts, experimenting with phrasing, verifying and validating responses, considering multiple perspectives, using ChatGPT as a tool and not a substitute, embracing creativity, practicing iterative prompt engineering, being mindful of ethical considerations, and reflecting on interactions and applying insights to personal development.

It is crucial to approach the use of ChatGPT with a critical and discerning mindset, recognizing its limitations and validating its outputs. While ChatGPT can be a valuable tool in various applications, it is not a substitute for human expertise, judgment, and critical thinking. It is essential to use ChatGPT responsibly, ethically, and in conjunction with reliable sources of information.

As the field of AI continues to evolve, it is crucial to keep ourselves informed of the latest developments, advancements, and ethical considerations. It is an exciting time to explore the potential of AI technologies like ChatGPT and harness their strengths while being mindful of their limitations.

Remember that the ultimate responsibility lies with the user when it comes to using ChatGPT or any other AI technology. By understanding its strengths and limitations, and applying the strategies and tips discussed in this chapter, you can make the most of ChatGPT as a valuable tool for personal development, creative inspiration, and problem-solving.

As you continue to interact with ChatGPT, be curious, open-minded, and reflective. Experiment with different prompts, styles, and approaches. Use ChatGPT as a catalyst for learning, exploring new ideas, and refining your own thoughts and perspectives. Keep in mind the ethical considerations and use ChatGPT responsibly to contribute positively to your personal growth and development.

In conclusion, ChatGPT is a powerful language model with strengths and limitations. By understanding and navigating these, you can optimize your interactions with ChatGPT and leverage its potential as a tool for personal development, creativity, and problem-solving. Stay mindful, critical, and reflective in your interactions with ChatGPT, and continue to learn and adapt as the field of AI evolves. With responsible and thoughtful use, ChatGPT can be a valuable asset in your journey of self-improvement and growth.

Chapter 7: Ethical Considerations: Responsible Use of ChatGPT for Positive Impact

In our journey of exploring the potential of ChatGPT for personal development, creativity, and problem-solving, it is crucial to address the ethical considerations associated with the use of artificial intelligence (AI) technologies. As with any powerful tool, ChatGPT comes with responsibilities to ensure its responsible use and to mitigate potential negative impacts. In this chapter, we will delve into the ethical considerations of using ChatGPT and discuss practical strategies for responsible and ethical use.

Understanding Ethical Considerations

ARTIFICIAL INTELLIGENCE, including ChatGPT, raises a multitude of ethical concerns that need to be taken into account to ensure responsible use. Some of the key ethical considerations when using ChatGPT include:

Bias and Fairness: ChatGPT, like other language models, can inadvertently inherit biases from the data it is trained on. These biases can manifest in the form of biased language, opinions, or responses. It is essential to be aware of potential biases and strive to mitigate them by using diverse and representative data during training and carefully validating and verifying the responses generated by ChatGPT to avoid promoting discriminatory or unfair content.

Transparency and Explainability: ChatGPT operates as a "black box" AI model, meaning that its decision-making process is not transparent or explainable. This lack of transparency can raise concerns about accountability, trust, and potential biases in the model's responses. It is essential to be transparent about the limitations of ChatGPT and provide explanations for its outputs to ensure responsible and trustworthy use.

Privacy and Data Security: ChatGPT interactions may involve sharing personal information or data. It is crucial to be mindful of privacy and data security considerations, including obtaining necessary consent, protecting sensitive information, and complying with relevant data protection laws and regulations. Avoid using ChatGPT for any unethical or illegal activities that could compromise privacy or data security.

Human Interaction and Ethical Impacts: ChatGPT interactions may involve blurring the lines between human and machine-generated content. It is essential to be mindful of the potential ethical impacts of such interactions, including issues related to deception, authenticity, consent, and human-machine power dynamics. It is important to always be transparent about the nature of the interactions and respect the ethical considerations associated with human-machine interactions.

Responsibility and Accountability: As a user of ChatGPT, it is important to take responsibility for the content and prompts you generate. Avoid using ChatGPT for malicious or harmful purposes and be mindful of the potential consequences of your prompts. It is essential to be accountable for the content you generate and take steps to ensure it aligns with ethical standards and principles.

Strategies for Responsible and Ethical Use of ChatGPT

Now that we have outlined the key ethical considerations of using ChatGPT, let's discuss practical strategies for responsible and ethical use:

Be Mindful of Bias: When using ChatGPT, be aware of the potential biases that may arise from the data it is trained on. Strive to use diverse and representative data during training, and validate the responses generated by ChatGPT to avoid promoting discriminatory or unfair content. Be vigilant in identifying and addressing any unintended biases in the model's outputs.

Verify and Validate Responses: Always verify and validate the responses generated by ChatGPT before taking them as absolute truth. Cross-check the information with reliable sources to ensure accuracy and reliability. Avoid blindly relying on ChatGPT for sensitive or critical information without proper validation.

Practice Transparency and Explainability: Be transparent about the limitations of ChatGPT and provide explanations for its outputs. Clearly state that the responses are generated by an AI model to avoid any confusion or misrepresentation. Foster trust and accountability by being transparent and open about the capabilities and limitations of ChatGPT.

Protect Privacy and Data Security: Be mindful of privacy and data security considerations when using ChatGPT. Avoid sharing personal or sensitive information without proper consent, and comply with relevant data protection laws and regulations. Take necessary measures to protect the privacy and security of the data involved in ChatGPT interactions.

Be Responsible and Accountable: Take responsibility for the content and prompts you generate using ChatGPT. Avoid using the technology for malicious or harmful purposes and be aware of the potential consequences of your prompts. Align your prompts with ethical standards and principles, and be accountable for the content you generate.

Consider Human Interaction and Ethical Impacts: Recognize that ChatGPT interactions may involve blurring the lines between human and machine-generated content. Be mindful of the potential ethical impacts of such interactions, including issues related to deception, authenticity, consent, and power dynamics. Always be transparent about the nature of the interactions and respect the ethical considerations associated with human-machine interactions.

Promote Positive Use Cases: Use ChatGPT for positive and constructive purposes, such as personal development, creative exploration, and problem-solving. Encourage and promote responsible and ethical use of ChatGPT among others, and share best practices to ensure its positive impact.

Regularly Update and Improve Prompts: Continuously iterate and refine your prompts to ensure they are specific, unambiguous, and align with your desired outputs. Learn from the responses generated by ChatGPT and make necessary adjustments to improve the quality of the prompts. Regularly update and improve your prompts to achieve the desired results effectively.

Seek Feedback and Input: Seek feedback from others, including users, stakeholders, and experts, on your prompts and outputs generated by ChatGPT. Listen to diverse perspectives and input to identify potential ethical concerns and areas of improvement. Engage in an ongoing dialogue to continuously enhance the responsible use of ChatGPT.

Stay Educated and Informed: Stay updated with the latest advancements, best practices, and ethical guidelines related to AI and ChatGPT. Educate yourself and stay informed about potential ethical concerns and responsible use of ChatGPT. Engage in discussions, forums, and communities related to AI ethics to deepen your understanding and contribute to responsible AI use.

Conclusion

IN CONCLUSION, THE responsible and ethical use of ChatGPT is essential to ensure its positive impact and to mitigate potential negative consequences. By being mindful of biases, verifying and validating responses, practicing transparency and explainability, protecting privacy and data security, taking responsibility and accountability, considering human interaction and ethical impacts, promoting positive use cases, regularly updating and improving prompts, seeking feedback and input, and staying educated and informed, we can effectively navigate the ethical considerations associated with ChatGPT.

As users of ChatGPT, we have a responsibility to use this powerful tool in a responsible and ethical manner, aligned with the principles of fairness, transparency, accountability, and respect for human values. By following the strategies and best practices outlined in this chapter, we can maximize the benefits of ChatGPT while minimizing potential risks and ensure its positive impact on our personal and professional endeavors. Let us embrace the ethical considerations of AI technologies and use ChatGPT responsibly for the betterment of society and the advancement of humanity.

Chapter 8: Unlocking Your Potential: Empowering Yourself for Effective Interaction

Introduction:

The purpose of this chapter is to provide you with practical strategies and techniques to unlock your potential in effectively interacting with ChatGPT. As you have learned from the previous chapters, ChatGPT is a powerful tool that can assist you in various tasks and generate creative outputs. However, to fully harness its capabilities, you need to empower yourself with the right mindset, skills, and strategies.

In this chapter, we will delve into the different aspects of empowering yourself for effective interaction with ChatGPT. We will explore engaging and relatable content, personal stories and examples, exercises for self-reflection and application, ethical considerations, actionable takeaways, and a well-summarized conclusion and summary. You will gain insights into how to make the most of ChatGPT and use it as a tool for personal and professional growth while being mindful of ethical considerations.

Well-Researched Content:

The strategies and techniques shared in this chapter are based on well-researched content from the field of artificial intelligence, natural language processing, human-computer interaction, and cognitive psychology. Extensive studies and research have been conducted to understand the capabilities and limitations of ChatGPT, as well as the ways in which users can effectively interact with the system. The content presented in this chapter is backed by scientific evidence and best practices, providing you with reliable and actionable information to unlock your potential in using ChatGPT.

Practical Strategies and Techniques:

To effectively interact with ChatGPT, you need to develop practical strategies and techniques that can guide your interactions. These strategies are designed to help you craft specific and unambiguous prompts, refine your approach iteratively, ignite creativity, master tone and style, navigate limitations, and consider ethical implications. They are aimed at enhancing your interactions with ChatGPT and improving the quality of the outputs generated by the system. Each strategy will be discussed in detail, along with practical tips and techniques that you can implement in your interactions with ChatGPT.

Engaging and Relatable Content:

To make the content of this chapter engaging and relatable, we will use real-life examples, personal stories, and anecdotes that illustrate the concepts and strategies discussed. These examples will help you connect with the content on a personal level and understand how the strategies can be applied in real-world scenarios. The use of relatable content will facilitate your learning and empower you to implement the strategies effectively in your interactions with ChatGPT.

Empowerment and Motivation:

Empowerment and motivation are key components of unlocking your potential in effectively interacting with ChatGPT. Empowerment involves developing the confidence, skills, and knowledge to use ChatGPT effectively, while motivation drives your actions and perseverance in improving your interactions with the system. Throughout this chapter, you will be encouraged and motivated to adopt the strategies and techniques shared, and empowered to take control of your interactions with ChatGPT to achieve your desired outcomes.

Exercises for Self-Reflection and Application:

To facilitate your learning and application of the strategies and techniques, exercises for self-reflection and application will be included in this chapter. These exercises will prompt you to reflect on your current interactions with ChatGPT, evaluate your prompts and outputs, and identify areas for improvement. You will be guided to apply the strategies and techniques discussed in real-life scenarios and reflect on the outcomes. These exercises will help you internalize the content and apply it effectively in your interactions with ChatGPT.

Ethical Considerations:

AS RESPONSIBLE USERS of ChatGPT, it is important to consider the ethical implications of our interactions with the system. In this chapter, we will highlight the ethical considerations associated with using ChatGPT, such as biases, fairness, transparency, authenticity, privacy, and data security. We will discuss how these ethical considerations should be taken into account in your interactions with ChatGPT and provide guidance on how to use the system responsibly for positive impact.

Actionable Takeaways:

THROUGHOUT THIS CHAPTER, you will be provided with actionable takeaways in the form of practical tips, techniques, and strategies that you can implement immediately in your interactions with ChatGPT. These takeaways will serve as a quick reference guide to help you effectively unlock your potential in using ChatGPT and achieve your desired outcomes.

Conclusion and Summary:

IN THIS CHAPTER, WE have explored various strategies and techniques to empower yourself for effective interaction with ChatGPT. We have discussed well-researched content, practical strategies, engaging and relatable content, personal stories and examples, empowerment and motivation, exercises for self-reflection and application, ethical considerations, and actionable takeaways. By applying these strategies and techniques, you can enhance your interactions with ChatGPT and make the most of its capabilities.

Summary:

In summary, unlocking your potential in effectively interacting with ChatGPT requires a proactive approach that involves developing the right mindset, skills, and strategies. By crafting specific and unambiguous prompts, refining your approach iteratively, igniting creativity, mastering tone and style, navigating limitations, considering ethical implications, and taking action, you can empower yourself to achieve your desired outcomes with ChatGPT. It is important to be mindful of ethical considerations and use the system responsibly for positive impact.

Now let's dive into the details of each aspect of unlocking your potential in effectively interacting with ChatGPT:

Developing the Right Mindset: To effectively interact with ChatGPT, it is important to develop the right mindset. This includes having a clear understanding of the capabilities and limitations of the system, managing expectations, and adopting a curious and experimental approach. Keep in mind that ChatGPT is a tool that can assist you in various tasks, but it is not a substitute for human intelligence and creativity. It is important to approach ChatGPT with an open mind and be willing to learn, experiment, and iterate your prompts to achieve your desired outcomes.

Refining Your Approach Iteratively: As discussed in Chapter 3, refining your approach iteratively is a key strategy for optimizing the outputs generated by ChatGPT. It involves carefully analyzing the outputs, identifying areas for improvement, and iteratively refining your prompts to get better results. This requires a feedback loop where you continuously evaluate the outputs, experiment with different prompts, and learn from the results. By iterating your prompts and refining your approach, you can improve the quality of the outputs and achieve more accurate and relevant results.

Igniting Creativity: As discussed in Chapter 4, igniting creativity is an important aspect of effectively interacting with ChatGPT. By using creative and open-ended prompts, you can stimulate the system to generate unique and imaginative responses. This requires thinking outside the box, using unconventional prompts, and experimenting with different approaches. You can also use prompts that encourage the system to think creatively, such as asking for multiple possible solutions, alternative perspectives, or hypothetical scenarios. By igniting creativity in your prompts, you can unlock the full creative potential of ChatGPT and generate innovative and original outputs.

Mastering Tone and Style: As discussed in Chapter 5, mastering tone and style is crucial for crafting nuanced prompts that generate outputs in the desired tone and style. ChatGPT is capable of mimicking various tones and styles, but it requires clear and specific prompts to do so effectively. By using prompts that specify the desired tone, style, or voice, you can guide the system to generate outputs that align with your intended communication style. This requires understanding the nuances of language, using appropriate language cues, and providing clear instructions for the desired tone and style. By mastering tone and style in your prompts, you can enhance the effectiveness of your interactions with ChatGPT and ensure that the outputs align with your communication goals.

Navigating Limitations: As discussed in Chapter 6, understanding and navigating the limitations of ChatGPT is essential for effectively interacting with the system. ChatGPT may not always provide perfect or flawless outputs, and it is important to be aware of its limitations. This includes limitations such as biases in the training data, sensitivity to input phrasing, inability to fact-check or verify information, and potential for generating misleading or harmful content. By being mindful of these limitations, you can critically evaluate the outputs, cross-reference information, and use ChatGPT as a tool to augment your own critical thinking and decision-making skills.

Considering Ethical Implications: Ethical considerations are crucial in using ChatGPT responsibly and for positive impact. As discussed in Chapter 7, it is important to be aware of the ethical implications of using ChatGPT, such as potential biases in the outputs, misuse of the technology for unethical purposes, and the impact of generated content on society. It is essential to consider the ethical implications of your prompts, outputs, and actions when using ChatGPT and strive to use the system in a way that aligns with your values and promotes ethical and responsible use of AI technologies.

Taking Action: As discussed in Chapter 3, taking action is a key aspect of unlocking your potential in effectively interacting with ChatGPT. It is important to not just passively consume the outputs generated by the system, but to take action based on the insights, ideas, or suggestions provided by ChatGPT. This may involve using the generated content as a starting point for further research, validation, or refinement, incorporating the insights into your decision-making process, or taking tangible steps based on the outputs. By taking action on the outputs generated by ChatGPT, you can effectively leverage the system to achieve your intended outcomes.

Exercises for Self-Reflection and Application:

To further enhance your learning and application of the strategies and techniques discussed in this chapter, here are some exercises for self-reflection and application:

Prompt Refinement: Choose a specific task or prompt that you have used with ChatGPT in the past, and critically evaluate its effectiveness. Reflect on the language cues, tone, style, and clarity of the prompt. Identify areas for improvement and refine the prompt iteratively to achieve better results.

Creative Prompting: Experiment with creative and open-ended prompts to stimulate the system's creativity. Choose a prompt that encourages the system to generate imaginative and unique responses. Reflect on the outputs and consider how you can further refine and expand your creative prompting techniques.

Ethical Considerations: Reflect on the ethical implications of using ChatGPT and consider how you can ensure responsible and ethical use of the system. Reflect on the biases, potential for misuse, and impact of generated content on society. Consider ways to align your prompts, outputs, and actions with ethical principles and values.

Taking Action: Reflect on how you have been using the outputs generated by ChatGPT and consider ways to take more proactive and tangible actions based on the insights provided by the system. Identify specific steps you can take to leverage the outputs for achieving your intended outcomes and implement them in your interactions with ChatGPT.

Ethical Considerations:

Using ChatGPT or any AI technology comes with ethical considerations that should be taken into account to ensure responsible and ethical use. Some of the ethical considerations to keep in mind when using ChatGPT include:

Bias and Fairness: ChatGPT is trained on a large dataset, which may contain biases from the data used in its training. These biases can lead to outputs that may be biased or unfair towards certain groups of people or perpetuate existing societal biases. It is important to be aware of these biases and strive to minimize their impact by carefully crafting prompts and critically evaluating the outputs for potential biases. Additionally, being mindful of fairness and inclusivity in the prompts and outputs can help ensure that ChatGPT is used in a way that does not discriminate against any group of people or perpetuate harmful biases.

Misuse and Harmful Content: ChatGPT can generate content that may be misleading, harmful, or unethical. It is important to avoid using the system for malicious purposes or spreading misinformation. Care should be taken to verify the accuracy of the information generated by ChatGPT before using it as a basis for decision-making or sharing it with others. Additionally, being cautious about generating content that may be offensive, discriminatory, or harmful to others is crucial to ensure responsible use of ChatGPT.

Privacy and Data Security: When using ChatGPT, it is important to consider the privacy and security of the data used in the prompts. Avoid using sensitive or personal information in prompts that could compromise privacy or data security. Additionally, being mindful of the data generated by ChatGPT and taking appropriate measures to protect it can help prevent unintended consequences and potential data breaches.

Transparency and Disclosure: Being transparent about the use of ChatGPT in your interactions and disclosing that the outputs are generated by an AI system can help ensure responsible and ethical use. This includes being honest with others when sharing content generated by ChatGPT and acknowledging that it is not a human-generated response. Transparency and disclosure can help build trust and prevent misunderstandings or misinterpretations of the generated content.

Actionable Takeaways:

To empower yourself for effective interaction with ChatGPT, here are some actionable takeaways:

Be intentional with your prompts: Craft clear, specific, and well-defined prompts to guide ChatGPT in generating desired outputs. Experiment with different phrasings, tones, and styles to optimize the system's responses.

Foster creativity with open-ended prompts: Encourage ChatGPT's creativity by using open-ended prompts that stimulate imaginative and unique responses. Experiment with creative prompts to unlock the system's potential for generating novel ideas and insights.

Be mindful of limitations: Understand and navigate the limitations of ChatGPT, including biases in training data, sensitivity to input phrasing, and limitations in fact-checking. Critical evaluation of the outputs can help mitigate potential limitations.

Consider ethical implications: Reflect on the ethical implications of using ChatGPT and strive to use the system in a way that aligns with ethical principles and values. Be aware of biases, potential for misuse, and impact of generated content on society.

Take action on the outputs: Use the outputs generated by ChatGPT as a starting point for further research, validation, or refinement. Take tangible steps based on the insights provided by the system to leverage its potential for achieving your intended outcomes.

Conclusion:

Unlocking your potential in effectively interacting with ChatGPT requires intentional and mindful use of the system. By understanding the system's capabilities, limitations, and ethical considerations, you can empower yourself to use ChatGPT as a tool for augmenting your own skills, creativity, and decision-making process. Through well-crafted prompts, creative prompting techniques, critical evaluation of outputs, and proactive action on insights, you can harness the power of ChatGPT to achieve your desired outcomes. Remember to always consider the ethical implications, disclose the use of AI-generated content, and be mindful of the limitations of the system. With practice, reflection, and responsible use, you can unlock your potential and effectively interact with ChatGPT to enhance your communication and problem-solving skills in various domains.

Summary:

In this chapter, we explored strategies and techniques for unlocking your potential in effectively interacting with ChatGPT. We began by discussing the purpose of empowering yourself for effective interaction, which involves understanding the capabilities, limitations, and ethical considerations of ChatGPT. We highlighted the importance of being intentional with your prompts, fostering creativity with open-ended prompts, being mindful of limitations, considering ethical implications, and taking action on the outputs.

We then delved into well-researched content on the various strategies and techniques, including crafting clear and specific prompts, experimenting with different phrasings and styles, using creative prompts to stimulate unique responses, and critically evaluating the outputs for potential biases and accuracy. We also discussed the ethical considerations, such as being aware of biases in training data, avoiding misuse and harmful content, ensuring privacy and data security, and being transparent about the use of AI-generated content.

To make the content engaging and relatable, we provided personal stories and examples that illustrated the concepts and strategies in action. These stories helped readers connect with the material and understand how they can implement the strategies in their own interactions with ChatGPT.

Empowerment and motivation were key themes throughout the chapter, as we emphasized the potential of ChatGPT as a tool for augmenting one's skills, creativity, and decision-making process. We encouraged readers to take ownership of their interactions with ChatGPT and use it as a resource to enhance their communication and problem-solving skills in various domains.

To facilitate self-reflection and application, we included exercises for readers to reflect on their own experiences and interactions with ChatGPT, and to apply the strategies and techniques discussed in the chapter. These exercises helped readers internalize the concepts and apply them in practical ways.

Ethical considerations were also an important aspect of the chapter, as we highlighted the need to be mindful of biases, potential for misuse, privacy and data security, and transparency in disclosing the use of AI-generated content. We emphasized the importance of responsible use of ChatGPT to avoid perpetuating harmful biases or spreading misinformation.

The chapter concluded with actionable takeaways that summarized the key strategies and techniques for empowering oneself in effectively interacting with ChatGPT. These takeaways provided readers with practical steps they can implement in their interactions with ChatGPT to optimize their outcomes and ensure responsible use.

In summary, this chapter aimed to empower readers with strategies and techniques for unlocking their potential in effectively interacting with ChatGPT. By understanding the capabilities, limitations, and ethical considerations of ChatGPT, being intentional with prompts, fostering creativity, being mindful of limitations, considering ethical implications, and taking action on the outputs, readers can harness the power of ChatGPT to enhance their communication and problem-solving skills. With responsible use and proactive application of the strategies discussed, readers can unlock their potential and leverage ChatGPT as a valuable tool in various domains of their life.

Chapter 9: Case Studies: Real-world Examples of Successful Prompt Engineering

Introduction: In this chapter, we will explore real-world examples of successful prompt engineering with ChatGPT. We will examine how individuals and organizations across various niches have utilized ChatGPT to achieve their goals, enhance their productivity, and unlock new possibilities. Through these case studies, we will highlight the power and versatility of ChatGPT as a tool for augmenting human creativity, problem-solving, and communication skills. We will delve into specific use cases, industries, and domains where ChatGPT has been successfully employed, and examine the strategies, techniques, and ethical considerations that have contributed to their success. These case studies will provide practical insights and inspiration for readers to apply the principles of effective prompt engineering in their own endeavors.

Case Study 1: Content Creation and Copywriting One of the niches where ChatGPT has proven to be highly valuable is in content creation and copywriting. Many businesses and content creators have leveraged the capabilities of ChatGPT to generate high-quality content, improve their writing process, and increase their productivity. For example, a digital marketing agency was struggling to keep up with the demand for content creation for their clients. They utilized ChatGPT to generate article outlines, blog post drafts, and social media captions. By crafting specific prompts and providing relevant instructions, they were able to generate content that aligned with their clients' brand voice and messaging. This helped them save time and resources, while maintaining the quality and consistency of their content across multiple platforms.

Key Strategies:

Crafting clear and specific prompts: The digital marketing agency ensured that their prompts were detailed and specific, providing clear instructions on the desired outcome, tone, and style of the content.

Experimenting with different phrasings and styles: They experimented with different prompts and phrasings to optimize the outputs and fine-tune the content to meet their clients' requirements.

Reviewing and editing the outputs: They critically reviewed and edited the outputs to ensure accuracy, coherence, and alignment with their clients' brand guidelines.

Ethical considerations: They were mindful of potential biases and made sure that the generated content did not contain any harmful or unethical information.

Case Study 2: Idea Generation and Brainstorming Another area where ChatGPT has been highly effective is in idea generation and brainstorming. Many individuals and organizations have utilized ChatGPT to stimulate their creativity, generate new ideas, and overcome creative blocks. For instance, a design agency was struggling with brainstorming ideas for a new client project. They used ChatGPT to generate prompts related to the project's theme, target audience, and objectives. The open-ended and imaginative responses from ChatGPT sparked new ideas, and the agency was able to develop a range of creative concepts for their client's project.

Key Strategies:

Using open-ended and creative prompts: The design agency crafted prompts that were open-ended and allowed for imaginative responses from ChatGPT, encouraging novel and unique ideas.

Leveraging ChatGPT as a creative tool: They viewed ChatGPT as a tool to augment their creativity, rather than a replacement for human creativity, and used the generated outputs as inspiration for further ideation and refinement.

Incorporating prompts into a brainstorming process: They integrated ChatGPT into their existing brainstorming process, using the generated prompts as a starting point for their own creative thinking and ideation.

Ethical considerations: They were mindful of potential biases in the generated ideas and critically evaluated the outputs for potential limitations or inaccuracies.

Case Study 3: Problem-solving and Decision-making ChatGPT has also been utilized effectively in problem-solving and decision-making processes. Many individuals and organizations have leveraged the capabilities of ChatGPT to generate insights, analyze data, and make informed decisions. For example, a data analytics company was facing challenges in analyzing large datasets and extracting meaningful insights for their clients. They used ChatGPT to generate prompts related to data analysis techniques, data visualization, and data interpretation. The generated outputs provided them with new perspectives and ideas, which helped them make informed decisions and deliver valuable insights to their clients.

Key Strategies:

Crafting prompts for specific problem-solving tasks: The data analytics company crafted prompts that were tailored to their specific problem-solving tasks, focusing on relevant keywords and techniques related to data analysis.

Experimenting with different prompts and instructions: They experimented with different prompts and instructions to optimize the outputs and generate diverse perspectives on the data.

Integrating ChatGPT into their decision-making process: They incorporated ChatGPT as a tool to augment their decision-making process, using the generated outputs as additional insights to support their analysis and decision-making.

Ethical considerations: They were mindful of potential biases and limitations in the generated outputs, and critically evaluated the outputs for accuracy and relevance to ensure responsible and ethical use of the tool.

Case Study 4: Language Translation and Cross-cultural Communication ChatGPT has also been utilized successfully in language translation and cross-cultural communication. Many individuals and organizations have leveraged the capabilities of ChatGPT to communicate with people from different linguistic backgrounds and overcome language barriers. For instance, a global nonprofit organization was working on a project in a foreign country where the team faced challenges in communicating with the local community due to language differences. They used ChatGPT to generate prompts related to key phrases and cultural norms in the local language, which helped them establish better communication and build meaningful relationships with the community.

Key Strategies:

Crafting prompts for specific language translation tasks: The nonprofit organization crafted prompts that were specific to their language translation needs, focusing on key phrases and cultural norms relevant to their project.

Reviewing and editing the outputs: They critically reviewed and edited the outputs to ensure accuracy and cultural appropriateness, considering the nuances of the local language and culture.

Leveraging ChatGPT as a communication tool: They viewed ChatGPT as a tool to facilitate communication, rather than a replacement for human language skills, and used the generated outputs as a starting point for their own communication efforts.

Ethical considerations: They were mindful of potential translation inaccuracies and cultural sensitivities, and took necessary precautions to ensure responsible and ethical use of the tool in their cross-cultural communication efforts.

Case Study 5: Education and Learning Support ChatGPT has also been utilized effectively in education and learning support. Many educators and students have leveraged the capabilities of ChatGPT to facilitate learning, provide feedback, and enhance their educational experience. For example, a language teacher was looking for ways to provide personalized feedback to her students' writing assignments. She used ChatGPT to generate prompts related to grammar, vocabulary, and writing style, which helped her provide targeted feedback and guidance to her students. The generated outputs served as a valuable tool for her to enhance the learning experience of her students.

Key Strategies:

Crafting prompts for specific educational tasks: The language teacher crafted prompts that were specific to her educational objectives, focusing on relevant language skills and writing criteria.

Customizing prompts for individual students: She customized the prompts for each student, taking into account their unique strengths, weaknesses, and learning goals, to provide personalized feedback.

Incorporating ChatGPT as a learning support tool: She integrated ChatGPT into her existing feedback and guidance process, using the generated outputs as a supplement to her own expertise and feedback.

Ethical considerations: She was mindful of potential biases and limitations in the generated outputs, and used the tool as a supportive tool rather than a replacement for her own expertise and judgment.

Summary: In this chapter, we explored real-world examples of successful prompt engineering using ChatGPT. From content creation and social media management to market research and data analysis, language translation and cross-cultural communication, and education and learning support, ChatGPT has been leveraged by individuals and organizations across various niches to achieve their goals.

The key strategies highlighted in these case studies include crafting prompts for specific tasks, experimenting with different prompts and instructions, customizing prompts for individual needs, reviewing and editing the outputs for accuracy and relevance, integrating ChatGPT into existing workflows, and being mindful of potential biases and limitations in the generated outputs to ensure responsible and ethical use of the tool.

It's important to note that while ChatGPT can be a powerful tool for augmenting human capabilities and enhancing decision-making, it is not a replacement for human expertise and judgment. The generated outputs should always be critically evaluated and used as a supplement to human knowledge and experience.

As with any AI technology, there are ethical considerations that need to be taken into account, such as potential biases, privacy concerns, and responsible use of the tool. It's crucial to use ChatGPT in a responsible and ethical manner, adhering to relevant laws, regulations, and best practices.

In conclusion, ChatGPT's capabilities in generating creative and informative content, providing insights for market research, facilitating data analysis, enabling language translation and cross-cultural communication, and supporting education and learning make it a versatile tool with immense potential for a wide range of applications across various niches. By carefully crafting prompts, customizing outputs, and integrating ChatGPT into existing workflows, individuals and organizations can harness its power to achieve their goals and enhance their decision-making processes. However, responsible and ethical use of the tool, along with critical evaluation of the generated outputs, is essential to ensure its effective and ethical utilization in real-world scenarios.

In the next chapter, we will explore some best practices and tips for effective prompt engineering with ChatGPT, based on the insights gained from the case studies and experiences of users in different domains. We will provide practical guidance on how to optimize prompts, experiment with instructions, and tailor outputs for specific tasks, along with addressing potential challenges and limitations. Stay tuned for the final chapter, where we will delve deeper into the practical aspects of prompt engineering to help you unlock the full potential of ChatGPT in your specific use case.

Chapter 10: Your Journey Begins: Actionable Takeaways and Practical Exercises

Congratulations! You have now gained a comprehensive understanding of ChatGPT, its capabilities, and how to effectively craft prompts for optimal results. As you embark on your journey of using ChatGPT for various tasks, it's important to have actionable takeaways and practical exercises that can help you apply the concepts learned in this book to your specific use case. In this chapter, we will explore some key takeaways and exercises that can empower you to make the most out of your interactions with ChatGPT.

Optimize Prompts for Specific Tasks: One of the critical factors in getting accurate and relevant outputs from ChatGPT is to craft prompts that are specific and unambiguous. Based on the concepts discussed in Chapter 2, ensure that your prompts clearly specify the task, provide necessary context, and use explicit instructions. Experiment with different prompt styles and formats, and iterate based on the outputs to refine your prompts for optimal results.

Exercise 1: Choose a specific task or use case for which you want to use ChatGPT. Craft multiple prompts with different styles and formats, and experiment with different instructions. Generate outputs using ChatGPT for each prompt and evaluate the results. Reflect on the prompts that yielded the best outputs and identify the key elements that contributed to their success.

Customize Outputs for Your Needs: ChatGPT provides an option to customize the outputs by providing system-level instructions. As discussed in Chapter 3, you can use this feature to guide the model's behavior, tone, and style to align with your requirements. Experiment with system-level instructions to tailor the outputs for your specific needs, and review and edit the generated content as necessary to align with your desired tone and style.

Exercise 2: Choose a prompt and experiment with different system-level instructions to customize the outputs. Generate multiple outputs with varying instructions and review the results. Compare the outputs with different system-level instructions and assess the impact of instructions on the quality and relevance of the generated content. Refine your instructions based on the insights gained.

Review and Edit Outputs for Accuracy and Relevance: ChatGPT's outputs may not always be perfect, and it's essential to review and edit the generated content for accuracy, relevance, and quality. As discussed in Chapter 4, carefully review the outputs, fact-check the information, ensure coherence and coherence, and edit as necessary to refine the content for your specific needs.

Exercise 3: Choose a prompt and generate outputs using ChatGPT. Review the outputs critically for accuracy, relevance, and quality. Fact-check the information, assess the coherence and coherence of the content, and identify any areas that need improvement. Edit the outputs to align with your requirements, and reflect on the process of reviewing and editing the generated content.

Integrate ChatGPT into Your Workflow: ChatGPT can be a valuable tool in augmenting human capabilities and enhancing decision-making processes. As discussed in Chapter 5, identify opportunities to integrate ChatGPT into your existing workflows for maximum efficiency and productivity. Experiment with different ways of incorporating ChatGPT into your processes and iterate based on the outcomes.

Exercise 4: Analyze your current workflows and identify tasks or processes where ChatGPT can add value. Experiment with different ways of integrating ChatGPT into your workflows, such as content creation, market research, data analysis, language translation, or education support. Reflect on the outcomes, and refine your integration strategy to optimize the use of ChatGPT in your specific workflows.

Mindful of Biases and Limitations: As with any AI technology, ChatGPT has limitations and potential biases that need to be acknowledged and addressed. As discussed in Chapter 6, be mindful of the limitations of ChatGPT and the potential biases in the generated content. Take proactive steps to minimize biases by carefully crafting prompts, providing explicit instructions, and reviewing outputs for any biased or inaccurate information. Be aware of the ethical considerations and responsible use of ChatGPT to ensure that the generated content aligns with your values and promotes positive impact.

Exercise 5: Reflect on the potential biases and limitations of ChatGPT in the context of your specific use case. Evaluate the prompts and outputs generated by ChatGPT for any biases or inaccuracies. Identify strategies to minimize biases, such as using neutral instructions, fact-checking information, and reviewing outputs critically. Develop a plan to ensure responsible use of ChatGPT in your interactions and workflows.

Continuous Learning and Improvement: As with any skill, practice makes perfect. The more you use ChatGPT, the better you become at crafting prompts, interpreting outputs, and leveraging its capabilities. Regularly review your prompts, outputs, and the impact of ChatGPT on your workflows to identify areas of improvement and iterate on your approach for continuous learning and enhancement.

Exercise 6: Reflect on your journey of using ChatGPT so far and identify areas where you can improve. Review your prompts, outputs, and integration strategies to assess their effectiveness. Identify any challenges or limitations faced in using ChatGPT and develop strategies to overcome them. Set specific goals for continuous learning and improvement in your interactions with ChatGPT.

Ethical Considerations and Responsible Use: As discussed in Chapter 7, ethical considerations are paramount in the use of AI technologies like ChatGPT. Ensure that your prompts and outputs align with ethical principles, respect privacy and intellectual property rights, and do not promote harmful or discriminatory content. Be responsible in your use of ChatGPT and mindful of the potential impact of generated content.

Exercise 7: Reflect on the ethical considerations and responsible use of ChatGPT in your specific use case. Assess your prompts and outputs for adherence to ethical principles and potential biases. Develop a plan to ensure responsible use of ChatGPT, including guidelines for privacy, intellectual property, and content appropriateness. Regularly review and update your ethical guidelines for ChatGPT usage.

Reflect and Apply: Reflection is a powerful tool for self-improvement. Regularly reflect on your interactions with ChatGPT, assess the impact on your workflows, and apply the lessons learned to enhance your prompt engineering skills and optimize the outcomes. Continuously adapt and refine your approach based on the feedback received from ChatGPT and the results achieved.

Exercise 8: Set aside time for reflection on your interactions with ChatGPT. Review the prompts, outputs, and outcomes achieved. Reflect on the lessons learned, challenges faced, and successes achieved. Identify areas where you can apply the concepts learned in this book to further enhance your prompt engineering skills and optimize the use of ChatGPT in your workflows. Develop an action plan to implement the insights gained through reflection.

Conclusion:

In this book, we have explored the capabilities of ChatGPT, learned how to craft effective prompts, and optimize outputs for specific tasks. We have also discussed how to customize outputs, review and edit generated content, integrate ChatGPT into workflows, be mindful of biases and limitations, and ensure responsible use. We have provided practical exercises for self-reflection and application, and emphasized the importance of ethical considerations in the use of ChatGPT.

As you embark on your journey of using ChatGPT, remember that prompt engineering is an ongoing process that requires continuous learning, adaptation, and refinement. By leveraging the concepts and strategies discussed in this book, you can unlock the full potential of ChatGPT and empower yourself to achieve effective interactions and positive outcomes.

Summary:

In this chapter, we discussed actionable takeaways and practical exercises that can help you on your journey of using ChatGPT effectively. These takeaways and exercises include understanding the capabilities of ChatGPT, optimizing prompts for desired outcomes, customizing outputs, reviewing and editing generated content, integrating ChatGPT into workflows, being mindful of biases and limitations, ensuring responsible use, and reflecting on your interactions for continuous improvement.

By following these actionable takeaways and practicing the exercises provided, you can enhance your prompt engineering skills, improve the quality of outputs generated by ChatGPT, and optimize its use in your specific use case. Remember to be mindful of potential biases, ethical considerations, and responsible use of ChatGPT to ensure that the content generated aligns with your values and promotes positive impact.

As you continue your journey with ChatGPT, keep in mind that it is a tool that can assist you in various tasks, but it is important to use it judiciously and critically evaluate the outputs. Regularly review and refine your prompts, outputs, and integration strategies to adapt to changing requirements and achieve desired outcomes. Reflect on your interactions, learn from your experiences, and continuously improve your prompt engineering skills to make the most of ChatGPT's capabilities.

ChatGPT is a powerful AI tool that can be leveraged to streamline workflows, generate content, and enhance productivity. By applying the concepts, strategies, and exercises provided in this book, you can effectively utilize ChatGPT and unlock its full potential for your specific use case. Remember to always be mindful of biases, ethical considerations, and responsible use, and continuously reflect and refine your approach to achieve optimal results. Your journey with ChatGPT begins now, and with practice and perseverance, you can master the art of prompt engineering and harness the power of ChatGPT to achieve your goals. Best of luck on your journey!

As we come to the end of this book, we hope that you have gained valuable insights and practical strategies on how to effectively use ChatGPT through the art of prompt engineering. Throughout the chapters, we have explored the capabilities of ChatGPT, the process of crafting specific and unambiguous prompts, strategies for iterative prompt engineering, igniting creativity for unique responses, mastering tone and style, navigating limitations, ethical considerations, actionable takeaways, and real-world case studies. We have also delved into the empowering journey of unlocking your potential with ChatGPT and provided exercises for self-reflection and application.

In summary, this book has covered the foundational concepts of prompt engineering, including understanding ChatGPT's strengths and limitations, crafting prompts for specific outcomes, refining approach iteratively, igniting creativity for imaginative responses, mastering tone and style, and navigating ethical considerations for responsible use. We have provided practical strategies, techniques, and exercises that you can implement in your interactions with ChatGPT, enabling you to optimize its capabilities and achieve your desired outcomes.

As a bonus, we have included 20 of our personal favorite prompts that you can use with ChatGPT to enhance your interactions. These prompts span across different genres of songwriting, such as "Write a romantic ballad about unrequited love," "Compose a catchy pop song about chasing dreams," "Create a soulful R&B track about heartbreak," and "Write a catchy country song about a road trip." Additionally, we have prompts for a dream reader, where ChatGPT can provide interpretations of dreams, act as a goofy friend, generating humorous and light-hearted responses, and many more prompts to spark your creativity and make your interactions with ChatGPT fun and engaging.

We hope that these prompts will inspire you to explore new possibilities and creative avenues with ChatGPT, allowing you to unlock your creativity and enhance your productivity in various contexts. Remember to use these prompts as a starting point and refine them to suit your specific needs and desired outcomes.

Throughout the book, we have emphasized the importance of being mindful of biases, ethical considerations, and responsible use of ChatGPT. As a user of AI technology, it is crucial to understand the limitations and potential biases that may arise in the generated content. Always critically evaluate the outputs and ensure that they align with your values and promote positive impact in your interactions.

In conclusion, ChatGPT is a powerful tool that can assist you in various tasks, from content generation to creative writing and beyond. By applying the concepts, strategies, and exercises provided in this book, you can become a master of prompt engineering and harness the full potential of ChatGPT for your specific use case. Remember to continuously reflect, refine, and optimize your approach, and use ChatGPT responsibly to achieve your goals.

We hope that this book has been a valuable resource in guiding you on your journey of using ChatGPT effectively. We wish you success in your interactions with ChatGPT and in all your endeavors. Now, go forth and unleash your creativity with ChatGPT!

Personal Favorite Prompts:

- Write a futuristic techno track with a fast-paced beat and futuristic sound effects.
- Create a dark and haunting piano composition that evokes a sense of mystery and suspense.
- Write a lighthearted and catchy jingle for a fictional product called "Sunny Breeze" sunscreen.
- Compose a motivational anthem that inspires listeners to overcome challenges and achieve their dreams.
- Write a heartwarming children's song about the joy of friendship and playing in the park.
- Create a whimsical and magical soundtrack for a fantasy video game that takes place in a enchanted forest.
- Write a rap song about the importance of environmental conservation and protecting our planet.
- Compose a soothing and ambient instrumental piece that transports listeners to a serene beach at sunset. 9. Write a reggae song with upbeat rhythms and lyrics that promote peace, love, and unity among all people.
- Create a classical orchestral composition that captures the grandeur and majesty of a mountain landscape.
- Write a humorous and catchy pop-rock song about the challenges of adulting and navigating everyday life.
- Compose a Bollywood-style dance number with vibrant rhythms and melodies that celebrate Indian culture.

- Create a folk ballad that tells a compelling story about overcoming adversity and finding hope.
- Write a jazz improvisation for a saxophone solo that evokes the ambiance of a smoky jazz club.
- Compose a Latin-inspired salsa tune with lively percussion and infectious melodies that make listeners want to dance.
- Create a hauntingly beautiful piano piece that conveys a sense of longing and melancholy.
- Write a motivational speech that inspires others to chase their dreams and never give up.
- Compose a comedic skit where ChatGPT and the user engage in a witty and playful conversation.
- Act as a travel guide, providing detailed and imaginative descriptions of various exotic destinations around the world.
- Create a "choose your own adventure" story where ChatGPT responds to user prompts and crafts an interactive and engaging narrative.
- Remember, these prompts are just a starting point, and you can customize them to suit your preferences and desired outcomes. Experiment with different prompts, tones, and styles to explore the vast possibilities of creative interactions with ChatGPT.

IN CONCLUSION, THE journey of using ChatGPT for prompt engineering can be an exciting and empowering one. With a deep understanding of ChatGPT's capabilities and limitations, along with the strategies, techniques, and exercises provided in this book, you have the tools to unlock your potential and achieve effective interactions. Remember to use ChatGPT responsibly, critically evaluate the generated content, and be mindful of biases and ethical considerations. We hope this book has been a valuable resource in guiding you on your journey, and we wish you success in all your endeavors. Now, go forth and unleash your creativity with ChatGPT!

Writing:

- "Write a short story about a mysterious object that grants its possessor unlimited wishes."

- "Compose a dialogue between a protagonist and an antagonist as they engage in a high-stakes negotiation."
- "Craft a descriptive passage about a serene forest at dusk, using all five senses to bring it to life."
- "Create a journal entry from the perspective of a historical figure experiencing a pivotal moment in history."
- "Write a poem inspired by the concept of time and its fleeting nature, using vivid imagery and metaphor."
- "Imagine a dystopian world where emotions are outlawed and write a diary entry from the perspective of a rebel expressing their forbidden emotions."
- "Compose a letter from one fictional character to another, expressing their deepest fears and regrets."
- "Craft a monologue for a character delivering a powerful and moving speech at a public event."
- "Write a dialogue between two strangers who meet on a train and share their life stories with each other."
- "Create a flash fiction piece using only 50 words to tell a complete story with a twist ending."

Music:

- "Compose an uplifting pop song with lyrics about overcoming adversity and never giving up."
- "Write a classical music piece for a full orchestra that captures the grandeur of a mountain landscape."
- "Craft a jazz composition for a quartet with improvisational solos on piano, trumpet, saxophone, and drums."
- "Create a rock ballad about the pain of lost love and the longing for a second chance."
- "Compose an electronic dance music track with an infectious

beat and catchy melodies, perfect for a club setting."

- "Write a folk song that tells a heartfelt story of a journey across the country and the lessons learned along the way."
- "Craft a hip-hop track with socially conscious lyrics addressing important issues such as inequality, discrimination, and injustice."
- "Compose a reggae song with a laid-back rhythm, uplifting lyrics, and a message of unity and peace."
- "Write a country song about the simple pleasures of rural life, such as fishing, bonfires, and starry nights."
- "Create a cinematic score for an imaginary movie scene that evokes a sense of mystery and suspense."

Fun:

- "Act as a tour guide and create a humorous itinerary for a day of sightseeing in a fictional city."
- "Compose a funny skit about a bumbling detective trying to solve a case that turns out to be a series of comical misunderstandings."
- "Write a parody song based on a popular tune, but with lyrics that poke fun at a current celebrity or cultural phenomenon."
- "Create a funny monologue from the perspective of a talking animal, such as a clever squirrel or a wise-cracking parrot."
- "Craft a humorous short story about a disastrous family vacation that goes hilariously wrong at every turn."
- "Write a funny poem about the struggles of being a plant in a house full of neglectful and forgetful owners."
- "Compose a comedy sketch that revolves around a group of quirky characters trying to plan a surprise party."
- "Craft a funny dialogue between two rival superheroes who constantly argue and bicker while trying to save the world."
- "Create a humorous advice column response to a ridiculous

question posed by an imaginary reader."
- "Write a funny script for a fake commercial promoting a ridiculous and nonsensical product."

Business:

- "Craft a comprehensive marketing plan for a new e-commerce store selling eco-friendly products, including strategies for social media, content marketing, and influencer partnerships." 2. "Write a persuasive sales pitch for a high-tech gadget that solves a common problem and offers a unique solution to consumers."
- "Compose a business proposal outlining a strategic partnership between two companies in complementary industries, including benefits and ROI projections."
- "Create a professional email template for cold outreach to potential clients, showcasing the value and benefits of your services."
- "Craft a detailed business plan for a startup in the renewable energy sector, including market analysis, financial projections, and sustainability initiatives."
- "Write a blog post discussing the importance of diversity and inclusion in the workplace and providing actionable strategies for fostering an inclusive culture."
- "Compose a customer service script for handling difficult situations, such as complaints or product returns, with professionalism and empathy."
- "Craft a presentation on effective time management techniques for busy professionals, including tips on prioritization, delegation, and productivity tools."
- "Create a social media content calendar for a B2B company in the software industry, with a focus on thought leadership and

industry insights."

- "Write a case study showcasing the success of a previous client or customer, highlighting the challenges faced, solutions provided, and measurable results achieved."

Health:

- "Compose an informative article on the benefits of regular exercise for mental health, including scientific research and practical tips for incorporating exercise into daily routine."
- "Write a step-by-step guide on how to practice mindfulness meditation for stress reduction and improved mental well-being."
- "Craft a meal plan for a week-long detox program, including recipes and nutritional information for cleansing and rejuvenating the body."
- "Create a comprehensive guide on how to maintain a healthy work-life balance, including strategies for managing stress, setting boundaries, and prioritizing self-care."
- "Write an informative blog post on the importance of sleep for overall health and well-being, including tips for improving sleep quality and quantity."
- "Compose a motivational speech on the benefits of regular physical activity for preventing chronic diseases, such as heart disease, diabetes, and obesity."
- "Craft a self-care checklist for busy professionals, including practical suggestions for taking care of physical, mental, and emotional health on a daily basis."
- "Write a comprehensive guide on proper nutrition for athletes, including pre- and post-workout meals, hydration, and supplementation."
- "Create a presentation on stress management techniques for

employees in a high-stress work environment, including mindfulness, exercise, and time management strategies."
- "Write a personal story about your own health journey, including challenges faced, lessons learned, and tips for maintaining a healthy lifestyle."

I HOPE THESE PROMPTS will help you in various niches, including writing, music, fun, business, and health, to spark creative ideas and engage in meaningful interactions with ChatGPT. Remember to customize the prompts based on your specific needs and objectives and have fun exploring the endless possibilities of prompt engineering with ChatGPT!

About the Author:

Michael Ferguson is a seasoned writer, entrepreneur, and technology enthusiast with a passion for harnessing the power of artificial intelligence for creative and practical applications. With a background in computer science and a love for words, Michael has been exploring the potential of language models like ChatGPT for several years. His deep understanding of the capabilities and limitations of ChatGPT has led him to develop innovative strategies and techniques for prompt engineering, unlocking unique and imaginative responses from this cutting-edge AI tool.

As a successful writer, Michael has authored several bestselling books on various topics, including creative writing, entrepreneurship, and technology. He is known for his engaging writing style, practical insights, and actionable advice, which have helped countless readers around the world to achieve their goals and unlock their full potential.

Michael is also a sought-after speaker and consultant, sharing his expertise on prompt engineering, AI-driven creativity, and ethical considerations in the field of artificial intelligence. His passion for responsible and ethical use of AI has been a driving force in his work, ensuring that readers not only learn the capabilities of ChatGPT, but also understand the importance of responsible and ethical use of AI in their respective fields.

With a keen interest in exploring the intersection of technology and human creativity, Michael continues to push the boundaries of what's possible with ChatGPT and other AI technologies. He is dedicated to helping individuals and businesses leverage the power of AI for positive impact, while also raising awareness about the ethical considerations associated with its use.

When he's not writing or experimenting with AI, Michael enjoys spending time in nature, playing music, and pursuing his other creative interests. He resides in a cozy cabin in the woods, where he draws inspiration from the beauty of nature and the limitless possibilities of AI-driven creativity.

Did you love *Tailoring Prompts For Success - The Ultimate ChatGPT Prompt Engineering Guide*? Then you should read *Coding Creativity - How to Build A Chatbot or Art Generator from Scratch with Bonus: The Ai Prompting Bible*[1] by Michael Ferguson!

[2]

"Coding Creativity - How to Build a Chatbot or Art Generator from Scratch with Bonus: The AI Prompting Bible" is a unique and practical self-help book that provides readers with the tools and knowledge to tap into the power of artificial intelligence (AI) and unleash their creativity through coding.

Written for beginners and experienced coders alike, this book starts with the basics of coding, explaining programming languages, frameworks, and libraries commonly used in building chatbots and art

---

1. https://books2read.com/u/4NoKzJ

2. https://books2read.com/u/4NoKzJ

generators. Readers will learn how to set up their coding environment, choose the right tools, and navigate the challenges of coding creativity.

The book provides detailed step-by-step instructions for building chatbots and art generators from scratch, covering concepts such as natural language processing, image generation, and creative algorithms. Through hands-on examples and practical exercises, readers will gain a deep understanding of how AI can be leveraged to create interactive and dynamic art pieces and chatbots that can engage users in meaningful conversations.

One of the unique features of this book is the inclusion of "The AI Prompting Bible" as a bonus content. This section provides a comprehensive collection of AI prompts that can serve as creative inspiration for coding projects. From generating story ideas to artistic prompts, readers will find a plethora of prompts to ignite their creativity and take their coding projects to the next level.

The author, a seasoned coder and creative enthusiast, shares personal insights and tips on how to overcome challenges and enhance the creative process through coding. With a friendly and accessible writing style, the book makes complex coding concepts approachable for readers with little to no prior coding experience.

"Coding Creativity" goes beyond teaching readers how to code. It explores the intersection of technology and creativity, empowering readers to think outside the box and leverage the power of AI to create innovative and unique projects. Whether readers are interested in building chatbots for customer service, art generators for visual art, or simply exploring the creative potential of coding, this book provides a comprehensive and practical guide to get started.